Table of C

MILLION DOLLAR WORDS

BY

Alan Brown

ABOUT THE AUTHOR

Alan Brown is a bid writer turned business strategist who helps people say what they really mean—clearly, confidently, and in a way that wins work. Over the last four years, his words have helped clients secure over $200 million in contracts, grants, and opportunities. He lives in the north of England with his long-suffering wife Hellen, six cats, a tortoise and is proud father to Callum, Leo, and Lauren.

READ THIS FIRST

You're about to read a book that's a little different.

Not because it's packed with complicated theories or clever tricks. But because it **works while you're reading it**.

Every page follows the same principles you're about to explore — clear, direct, outcome-focused. That means you'll be experiencing Million Dollar Words in action before you've even decided to try them for yourself.

You don't need to overthink it.
Just notice what makes certain sentences feel sharper, simpler, or more persuasive than you're used to.

When a line makes you stop, nod, or think *"That's good"* — that's the method at work.

By the time you reach the last page, you'll know how to create that same effect in your own words.

PREFACE

I didn't write this book to tell my story.

You won't find many personal anecdotes here. No origin tale. No dramatic turning point. That's not what this is for. That book may come later. This one has a different job.

This book was written because something practical needed to exist — something that helps good people say what they do in a way that works. Something that bridges the gap between "we're great at what we do" and "we keep being overlooked."

Million Dollar Words isn't about clever language. It's not about branding or storytelling. It's not even about writing, in the traditional sense. It's about communication that gets you chosen — by the right people, for the right reasons.

This book was shaped by years of working behind the scenes. Winning work for businesses large and small. Seeing what language moves people to action, and what language gets ignored. And over time, realizing that these tools weren't just for tenders or pitches — they could be used by anyone trying to grow something real.

It's not a copywriting manual.

It's not a marketing blueprint.

It's not a treatise on how to beat the algorithms.

It's a tool for clarity — because when people understand what you do, they're far more likely to choose you.

If that sounds useful, then you're in the right place.

Let's begin.

To Hellen —

For your patience, your strength, and your belief in me, even when I doubted myself.

For holding everything together so I could chase strange ideas.

This book wouldn't exist without you. Thank you.

INTRODUCTION

Read this first. Then read everything else. In order.

Words matter. You already know that.

But in business, they matter more than most people realize.

The right words can win contracts, unlock funding, attract dream clients, and open doors you didn't even know were shut.

The wrong words? They can cost you deals you were perfect for—and you'll never even know why.

This book is called Million Dollar Words for a reason. Because the techniques, tools, and principles inside it have helped me win my clients $million's in real business.

Not clicks. Not views. Not likes.

Revenue. Results. Contracts. Clients. Sales.

More importantly, these same principles helped me win those clients in the first place.

While I have said in the preface that this book isn't about me, I'll allow myself one story.

The seed of what became this book was planted years ago, by someone who probably didn't realize how much impact a small piece of advice would have.

I was working on a carefully written paper, overly polished—and my then-manager, mentor, and now close friend Gordon Riddell looked over it and said, almost as an instruction:

"Take out the word 'significant.'"

When I asked why, he calmly explained that if something couldn't be measured or defined, it didn't belong in a document designed to persuade.

I understood. And I didn't use it again.

That one moment quietly shaped everything you'll read in this book.

Yes, I've worked as a professional bid writer.

Yes, I've written hundreds of proposals, tenders, funding bids, and award entries—many of them in high-stakes situations where the difference between winning and losing came down to a single sentence.

But what matters here is what you do next.

Because this isn't just a book to read. It's a book to use.

What This Book Is Really About

Million Dollar Words isn't a thesaurus.
It's not about swapping weak words for stronger ones, although we'll do that.
It's not about clever copywriting tricks, although you'll learn a few of those too.

This book is about the psychology of communication in business, why some messages land with impact and others disappear into thin air. Why some businesses stand out without shouting, while others blend into the background even when they're brilliant.

It's about the words you choose and the way you choose them.
The structure.
The sequence.
The method behind the message.

It's about being clear when everyone else is vague.
Being direct when others are dressing things up.
Saying things simply—even when it feels uncomfortable—because simplicity is often more revealing than we realize.

We hide in complexity.
It gives us a way to sound professional without committing to anything.
But the moment you start speaking clearly, directly, honestly…
something shifts.
People lean in.
They get it.
They trust you.
They say yes.

That's what this book is for.

These aren't theories. They've been testing live pitches, real bids, urgent deadlines.
One business I worked with changed just a single sentence in a tender and went on to win a six-figure contract. That's the level of precision we're dealing with here.

What This Isn't

Let's be clear about something early on:
This isn't a copywriting book.
It's not a marketing book either.
Those are different disciplines.

Traditional marketing is often about reach. Visibility. Getting attention.
It casts a wide net. It builds brand. It creates awareness.
It has room to breathe, space to entertain, and time to warm people up.

Copywriting, as it's usually taught, sits somewhere between storytelling and sales.
It hooks. It persuades. It dances a little.

That's not what this book is about.

Million Dollar Words doesn't live in that world of soft edges and open loops.
It lives where decisions are made.
Where money changes hands.
Where you're asking someone to choose you—and mean it.

The words you'll learn here are designed for precision, not performance.
They don't exist to decorate a website or warm up an audience.
They exist to land a message, answer a brief, make a case, win the work.

We're not casting a net. We're sharpening a spear.

This isn't about "adding personality" or "finding your voice."
You've already got a voice. We're going to help it cut through.

So, while these techniques can absolutely improve your marketing and sales copy, they come from a different place.
They're rooted in clarity.
In logic.
In trust.
And most of all—in outcomes.

Because when you're asking someone to say yes to what you offer, you don't need to be flashy.
You need to be understood.

Not About Storytelling Either

Another idea worth addressing early—this isn't a book about storytelling.

In marketing circles, storytelling gets a lot of attention. And rightly so, it can be powerful when you have the time, space, and attention to build an emotional journey.

But that's not what Million Dollar Words is about.

This book isn't about weaving narrative arcs or painting vivid scenes. Because in most contexts we're writing for—proposals, bids, sales documents, funding applications—there's simply no room for it.

The reader isn't looking to be entertained.
They're looking for clarity.
For confidence.
For proof that you understand their problem and can solve it—fast.

That doesn't mean we never use story.
But when we do, it's controlled.
Tightly focused.
Tethered directly to the result the client cares about.

A well-structured case study is the best example. It tells a kind of story—but not one about you. It's a story that mirrors the client's situation.
It shows the problem they're facing.
What you did.
What happened next.
And most importantly—what that means for them.

It's not storytelling for the sake of color. It's relevance through example.
That's a different skill entirely.

So, while some of the techniques in this book may look like storytelling, they're not here to entertain.
They're here to land.
To persuade.
To help the right people say yes.

Read It in Order. For a Reason.

This isn't a 'dip in and out' kind of book.
Every Chapter builds on the last.
You'll learn new tools, then go back and see earlier ideas more clearly.
You'll realize that what seemed simple at the start was the foundation for something much more powerful.

And yes, you'll see some ideas more than once.
That's not an accident. That's how mastery works.

Some of the most effective tools in this book are deceptively simple—so simple that if I only mentioned them once, you'd probably skip past them.
But they're powerful.
And when you learn to use them properly, they'll change the way you write, pitch, sell, and speak.
They'll become second nature—and that's when they really start working for you.

So, when something sounds familiar, lean in—not away.
The repetition is deliberate.
It's there to sharpen your skills and embed the ideas so deeply that they show up when you need them most.

This Is About Written Words… But Not Only

Most of what we'll focus on is the written word.
Emails. Proposals. Web pages. Social posts. Sales decks. Offers.

Applications.
But the lessons don't stop there.

Once you learn how to write more clearly, you'll start to speak more clearly too.
You'll explain what you do with more confidence.
You'll pitch better.
You'll have stronger conversations.
You'll think more sharply—because writing is thinking made visible.

So yes, this book is about words on a page.
But the effect reaches far beyond that.

A Word About You

Maybe you're just starting out.
Maybe you've been in business for years.
Maybe you're great at what you do—but struggle to explain it.
Maybe you've got something incredible, but people just don't seem to get it.

Good.
You're in the right place.

This book will help you show the real value of what you offer.
Not by shouting louder.
Not by overpromising.
But by making your message impossible to ignore.

You'll learn to shift the conversation from price to impact.
From what you do to what it means.
From talking about yourself to talking about what really matters to your client.

You'll learn to package what you offer in a way that makes people want to say yes.

And you'll learn how to do it all without hype, nonsense, or manipulation, just clear, honest, powerful communication that works.

Do the Work

There are **exercises** in this book.
They're not optional.
They're how you go from learning this stuff to using it.

So, when you see one—stop.
Do it.
Write it out.
Try it on your own business.
You'll thank me later.

This isn't theory.
This is practice.
And when you do the work, you'll start seeing results quickly—because most businesses are still hiding in vague words and empty promises.
You won't be.

Most people don't write clearly because they're scared to.
Scared of being judged. Scared of being held to it.
But clarity is power.
The more clearly you say what you mean, the more seriously people take it.

A Note on AI

Let's address something else before we begin.

There's no denying that AI is changing the way we write.
It's fast. It's impressive. It can churn out content by the page, the post, or the paragraph in seconds.

And yes—it has a place.
It's a useful tool. I use it myself.
But tools don't replace intent.
They don't replace judgment.
And they don't replace the kind of clarity that comes from knowing what you're trying to say.

Authentic writing, the kind that moves people to action—doesn't come from autocomplete.
It comes from being sure of your message.
From putting the reader first.
From thinking clearly and saying something real.

That's not about being poetic. It's about being honest.
And that's something only a human can do.

So, if you're using AI in your writing—and you probably will—use it wisely.
Use it to draft, to brainstorm, to speed things up.
But don't expect it to think for you.
Because what makes writing effective isn't the words it contains.
It's the clarity behind them.

Million Dollar Words will give you that clarity.
And no machine can do that for you.

Let's Begin

This book was written for a reason.
Every Chapter has a job to do.
Every concept has a purpose.
And everything in here has been tested in the real world—by me, by my clients, and by business owners across dozens of industries.

So, if you're ready to show up with clarity, confidence, and credibility…
If you want your message to land, stick, and move people to action…
If you want to grow your business by being understood instead of overlooked…

Then turn the page.
Let's find your Million Dollar Words.

And once you do, people will see you differently.
Not just as a good option—
As the right choice.

WHY YOU'RE NOT BEING CHOSEN (YET)

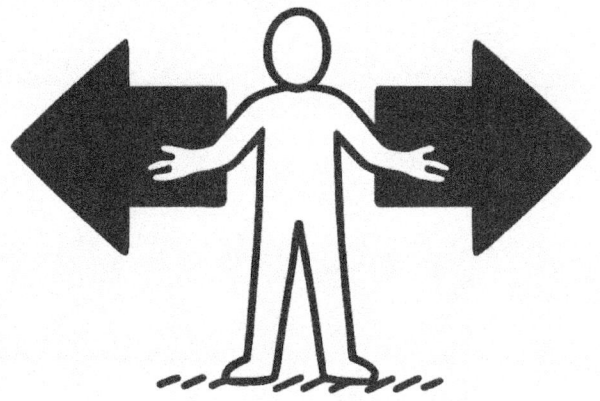

CHAPTER 1

The real reason your work isn't winning attention, trust, or sales — and what to do about it

1. The Invisible Problem

You do good work.
You've got real experience.
You care. You show up. You deliver.

But people don't "get" it.
Not quickly, anyway.

You've seen it happen:

The blank look during a pitch.

The unanswered quote.

The polite nod followed by radio silence.

You explain what you do, and people say, "Sounds good — I'll think about it."
But they don't.
They just move on.

They didn't say no.
They just didn't feel enough to say yes.

2. The Mistake You're Probably Making

Most people think the solution is to do more.

More information.
More credentials.
More features.
More bullet points.
More effort.

But more isn't better.

Clearer is better.

Here's the truth most business owners never hear:

It's not your work that's unclear. It's your words.

The way you talk about what you do is either:

Easy to understand… or hard to process.

Relevant to them… or all about you.

Sharp and memorable… or vague and forgettable.

And if your message feels vague, complex, or generic — people default to:

Price comparisons

Gut decisions

Or worse… nothing at all.

3. The Cost of Being Misunderstood

When people don't understand what you do, you pay the price.

You get filtered out.
Compared on price.
Left chasing.
Left explaining again.
Left wondering why people "don't get it."

You might assume you're not confident enough.
Or persuasive enough.
Or experienced enough.

But that's not it.

You don't need to shout louder. You need to say it better.

And that starts here.

4. What's Really Happening in Their Head

When someone reads your quote, your website, or your offer, they're thinking three things:

Do I understand this?

Is this for someone like me?

Does this feel worth my time or money?

If they hesitate on any one of those, you've lost them.

Not because they weren't interested.
But because something didn't click.

And once that moment passes, it's hard to get back.

5. What Being "Chosen" Really Means

This book isn't about sounding better.

It's about getting chosen.

To be chosen, someone must:

Understand what you do

See that it matters to them

Feel confident you can deliver

Believe the price makes sense

They don't need a show. They don't need a slogan.
They just need to get it — and trust it.

That's the power of clear, confident, useful language.

6. You're Not Alone

The people who struggle most with clarity are often the most capable.

They've got years of experience.
They've learned to improvise, adapt, solve problems.
They do the work — but struggle to describe the value of that work.

Why?

Because they're too close to it.
They know too much.
They assume others see what they see.

That's called the curse of knowledge — and we'll tackle it later.
But for now, just know: if this feels familiar, you're not broken.
You're just missing the structure.

And that's what this book will give you.

7. What You'll Start Noticing

Once you start seeing how language shapes decision-making, you can't unsee it.

You'll spot:

Empty words on competitors' websites

Wasted lines in your old proposals

Vague testimonials that could be gold with the right framing

Sales calls that get stuck in the mud because no one said what needed to be said

You'll also start rewriting things in your head:

"Don't say fast and reliable service. Say on-site in 48 hours with a fixed quote upfront."

"Don't say bespoke packages. Say choose from three clear service levels — all with built-in guarantees."

"Don't say we care about quality. Say every job gets a 12-month workmanship warranty."

These are small shifts.
But they have big consequences.

They move you from vague to vivid.
From general to grounded.
From being ignored to being remembered — and respected.

8. This Book Is Your Toolkit

This isn't a theory book.

It's a toolkit for making your message work harder — across everything you do:

Quotes

Websites

Proposals

Introductions

Emails

Sales conversations

Even how you answer the question: "What do you do?"

Each Chapter will show you:

A common problem in business messaging

What it sounds like

Why it's not working

What to do instead

Real phrases, prompts, and structures you can use right now

Some of these tools will feel almost too simple.

That's a good sign.

Powerful language doesn't come from sounding smart.
It comes from sounding clear.

Exercise: The Wall of Lost Sales

Let's start with some honest reflection.

Grab a notepad or blank document. Write down:

Three proposals or quotes you sent that didn't win.

Three emails or conversations where the client went quiet.

One time someone misunderstood what you offer.

Now ask yourself:

Did I explain the outcome clearly enough?

Did I focus too much on features and not enough on benefits?

Did the message make it easy for someone to say yes?

Don't worry about being perfect.
We'll come back to these examples later — and rewrite them together.

Where We Go From Here

Now that you know the real problem — unclear messaging — we can start solving it.

And we're not doing it randomly.

We're doing it with structure.

That's what the next Chapter is about — a model you'll use repeatedly.

It's called:

Position, Package, Propose.

It's simple. It's powerful. And once you have it, everything starts to make more sense.

Let's go there next.

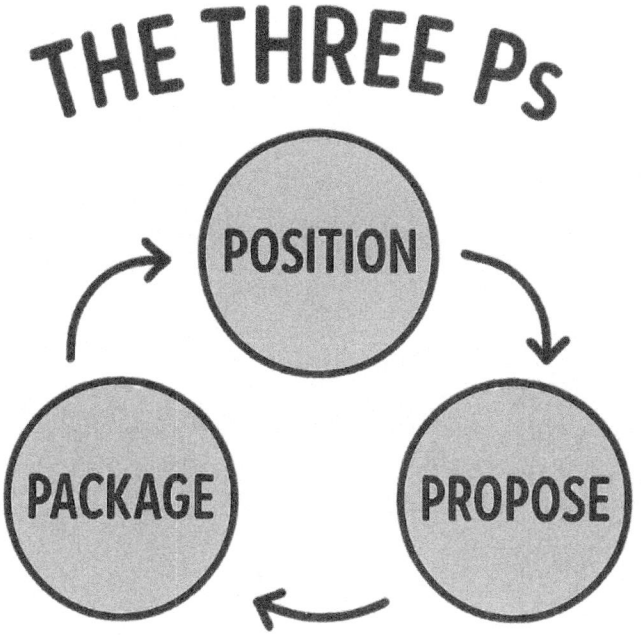

CHAPTER 2

A simple structure that makes everything you say clearer, stronger, and more compelling

1. Why We Need a Structure

If Chapter 1 revealed the real problem — not being understood — then this Chapter gives you the structure to fix it.

Because here's the first truth:

Most businesses don't need more content.
They need a way to organize their message, so people care.

Without a structure, your message rambles.
You start with the wrong detail.
You give too many options.
You talk about things that matter to you, not them.

But with a structure, you do the opposite:

You say the right thing, in the right order

You make the value feel obvious

You guide someone naturally toward a yes

That's what the Three Ps give you.

2. The Three Ps: An Overview

Here's the model we'll use throughout this book:

Position → Package → Propose

These aren't stages of business growth.
They're stages of communication — a way to build clarity into everything you say.

Let's break them down.

Position — How you are seen

This is the lens people look through when they encounter you.

It answers questions like:

Who are you for?

What space do you occupy in their mind?

Why would someone pay attention to you — now?

If your positioning is vague or confusing, nothing else will work.

If people don't believe you're relevant, they won't listen.
If they can't place you, they won't trust you.

That's why position is always first.

Package — What you offer and how it's framed

This is the part most businesses rush through or skip entirely.

Packaging answers:

What exactly do you do?

How is it structured?

What's included — and not included?

Why does this make sense for someone like me?

If your offer feels unclear or overwhelming, people hesitate.

If your pricing feels random or your service feels loose, people assume risk.

Good packaging creates certainty.

It makes your offer feel easier to say yes to.

Propose — How you ask

This is where the opportunity is often lost.

You've got their attention.
You've shown the value.
And then you say…

"Let me know what you think."

"Just wanted to follow up."

"Here's the price — any questions?"

That's not a proposal. That's hesitation.

A good proposal is:

Clear on the next steps

Framed around their outcomes

Backed by proof and confidence

Written in a way that invites action

When done well, a strong proposal closes the gap between interest and decision.

It's the difference between a maybe and a yes.

3. Why This Model Works

Most business communication fails because it's backwards.

We start by talking about ourselves — "We offer X, Y, Z."
Then we try to sell the detail — "Here's our price."
Then we panic — "Let me know if you have any questions!"

It's upside-down.

Instead, we flip it:

Start with their world → Position

Make your offer make sense to them → Package

Present the next step with clarity and confidence → Propose

This is how real decisions get made.

This is how you win trust and action without needing to push.

4. This Works Everywhere

Once you see this structure, you'll spot it everywhere.

You can use the 3 Ps to:

Restructure a homepage

Rewrite a quote

Rethink a pitch deck

Reorder a LinkedIn profile

Reframe a sales call

Rework your pricing

You'll never again be stuck thinking, "What do I say?"
You'll just ask:

How am I being positioned here?

Is the package clear?

Am I actually proposing anything?

And if any one of those is missing, you'll know exactly what to fix.

5. What It Feels Like When You Get It Right

When your message follows the 3 Ps, you get a different reaction.

People nod.
They say, "That makes sense."
They forward your proposal to the decision-maker without rewriting it.
They book the call. They say yes.
They stop asking for discounts.

You feel more confident, too — because you're not "winging it" anymore.
You're guiding people through a structured decision.

And that shows up in your language.
You sound clearer.
You ask better questions.
You answer objections before they happen.

You don't need to be a natural seller.
You just need a system that works.

Exercise: Find the Missing P

Let's put this into action.

Pick one of the following:

Your latest proposal or quote

Your homepage or LinkedIn summary

A sales email you recently sent

Now ask:

Is the Position clear?

Can they tell who it's for, and why they should care?

Is the Package structured?

Can they see what they get, how it works, and why it makes sense?

Is there a real Propose?

Have you clearly told them what to do next, and why?

Circle the P that's weakest.

That's your next rewrite.

(We'll return to this in the exercises later — so keep it handy.)

You've just seen the three Ps explained in the same style you'll soon be able to shape for yourself. Consider this your first real glimpse of how the approach works in practice.

Where We Go From Here

Now that we have the structure, we're going to spend the next three Chapters breaking it down — one P at a time.

We'll start with the one most people overlook:

Position — how to be seen the right way.

Because if you don't get seen the right way, the rest won't matter.

Let's fix that next.

CHAPTER 3

You might be brilliant — but if no one sees you the right way, it doesn't matter.

Position is what people think you do, and whether they believe it's valuable.

Whether we want to accept it or not; most businesses are invisible. Not because they're bad, but because they haven't made it clear what they are, who they're for, or why they matter.

This Chapter will fix that. Fast.

Why your business is getting filtered out, misunderstood, or ignored — and how to fix it

1. You're Already Being Positioned

Let's start with a hard truth::

People are already forming a position for you — whether you shape it or not.

Every sentence you write…
Every way you describe what you do…
Every line on your website, profile, quote, or brochure…

It all adds up to a position.

Not a tagline. Not a logo.
A mental shortcut — a fast judgment someone makes about you before they decide whether to go further.

That shortcut decides:

Whether they pay attention

Whether they think "this is for me"

Whether they trust you

Whether they ever click, reply, or buy

If you're not positioning yourself on purpose, you're being positioned by accident.

And accidental positioning is almost always weak.

2. Position Is Perception

Positioning is not about your job title.
It's not about where you rank in Google.
It's not about sounding impressive.

It's about how you are perceived — in a moment, by someone else.

Are you a premium service… or a generic one?

Are you relevant… or just background noise?

Are you trusted… or unproven?

The answer depends not just on what you do — but how you talk about it.

The same work can sound high-value or low-value, depending entirely on the language.

"We help landlords stay compliant with EPC and EICR regulations…"
sounds very different from:
"We do electrical testing and rewiring for buildings."

The work might be the same.
But the positioning is miles apart.

One makes you sound like a strategic partner.
The other makes you sound like another name in a spreadsheet.

3. The Default Position Most Businesses Fall Into

Without strong positioning, most businesses end up sounding like this:

"We offer a wide range of services tailored to meet your needs."

This sounds safe. Professional. Flexible.

It's also the fastest way to become invisible.

Why?

Because it positions you as:

Generic

Replaceable

Low trust

Low urgency

If someone doesn't know what makes you different, they'll assume you're the same as everyone else.
And when everyone sounds the same, price becomes the only differentiator.

That's when the race to the bottom begins.

4. How to Reclaim Your Position

Strong positioning starts with three questions:

Who is this for?
Be brave enough to be specific.
If you say "everyone," you sound like "no one."

What problem are they facing — right now?
Don't speak to their dreams. Speak to their pain, pressure, or friction.

Why are you the safe, obvious choice?
Not the only choice. The safe one. The one that makes them say,
"This makes sense. Let's talk to them."

You're not trying to convince.
You're trying to create clarity and relevance — fast.

Let's break those three down.

5. Who Is This For?

You've heard it before: niche down, pick a target audience, define your ideal client.

That's not just marketing advice. It's positioning in action.

Because the more clearly someone sees themselves in your words, the more likely they are to choose you.

"We help businesses" → vague
"We help local trades win commercial contracts" → clear
or
"We help domestic cleaners move into Airbnb and end-of-tenancy work" → precise and powerful

It's not about narrowing your entire business.
It's about speaking clearly to the people most likely to say yes.

Clarity is not limitation — it's magnetism.

6. What Problem Are They Facing?

People don't buy services.
They buy relief. Outcomes. Safety. Solutions.

Good positioning doesn't start with features — it starts with frustrations.

What's the pain they're trying to solve?
What's the fear they want to avoid?
What's the situation they're stuck in?

When you speak directly to that problem, something powerful happens:

They stop skimming. They start listening.

"Still chasing unpaid invoices? We help contractors get paid in 7 days or less."

"Struggling to sell your home? We help sellers get market-ready without agents or drama."

"Losing tenders you know you could deliver? We'll help you win the next one — with words that work."

Your work becomes relevant. And relevance is the fastest path to trust.

7. Why You're the Safe, Obvious Choice

People are not looking for the best.
They're looking for something that feels like a safe decision.

And safety comes from:

Clarity (they understand you)

Familiarity (you speak their language)

Proof (you've done it before)

Framing (you've positioned yourself well)

A buyer wants to feel two things:

35

"I get what you do."
"You've done this before — for people like me."

That's what strong positioning gives them.

8. Examples of Clear Positioning

Let's look at a few pairs — one vague, one clear:

"We build websites for small businesses."
"We build 3-page websites for trades who want more calls — not more clicks."

"We help people with their mindset."
"We help self-employed dads who feel stuck — and want a plan to move forward."

"We offer virtual assistant services."
"We help solo business owners delegate 10 hours of admin per week — without hiring full-time."

In each case, the second version:

- Says who it's for
- Names the outcome
- Makes the reader feel seen

That's what positioning sounds like.

Exercise: Fix Your Positioning Statement

Write your current intro, tagline, or first sentence from your website or social media bio.

Now run it through this test:

Is it specific? (Who is this for?)

Is it relevant? (What problem or outcome is mentioned?)

Is it safe? (Does it feel like a low-risk choice to explore?)

Now try rewriting it using this simple format:

"We help [specific audience] who are [problem/situation] — so they can [benefit/outcome]."

Examples:

"We help landlords with multiple properties reduce energy waste — so they can stay compliant and cut costs."

"We help small construction firms win council contracts — so they stop losing tenders they know they could deliver."

Try two or three variations. Test the language.
You'll feel when it lands.

9. What Changes When You Get This Right

With clear positioning:

Your proposals start stronger

Your emails get replies

Your quotes feel like solutions

Your homepage becomes a filter — not a brochure

You stop attracting bad-fit clients

You start attracting better ones — because they get what you do

This is how your message becomes a magnet — not a megaphone.

And this is only the first piece.

Where We Go From Here

Now that people see you the right way, the next step is to make your offer make sense.

That means structuring what you do in a way that feels easy to buy, simple to explain, and safe to say yes to.

That's where we go next:

Chapter 4: Package — Make What You Do Make Sense

Let's turn clarity into confidence — and build offers people want.

PACKAGE

EASY TO CHOOSE

CHAPTER 4

If what you sell doesn't make sense — people won't buy it.

Package isn't about how your offer looks. It's about how well it lands in someone else's head.

Confused buyers don't buy. And most businesses are selling services in ways that sound confusing, overwhelming, or vague.

Let's fix that, so people say: "Yes, that's exactly what I need."

How to turn your skills and services into clear, structured offers that people want to say yes to

1. The Problem with the Way Most Offers Are Presented

Most businesses don't have a clear offer.

They have a list of tasks.
Or a set of bullet points.
Or a vague promise of results.

And so, when someone asks, "What exactly do I get?", the answer is... unclear.

That leads to:

Confused prospects

Distrust around pricing

Wasted sales conversations

Unclear expectations

Hesitation to commit

Because if you aren't clear about what you're offering, your client will fill in the blanks — and they'll usually assume the worst:

"Is this going to drag on?"
"What exactly am I paying for?"
"Is this worth it?"

Your offer should remove that uncertainty — not create it.

2. What Packaging Actually Means

Packaging is how you present and structure what you do.

It's not about adding ribbons or fancy names.
It's about creating clarity and confidence.

When done well, a well-packaged offer:

Feels valuable

Looks complete

Creates a clear path to the outcome

Justifies the price

Makes it easier to say yes

Think of it like building a shelf:

You don't just hand someone a pile of parts.

You give them a box with a clear picture, a list of contents, a step-by-step process, and a promise of the end result.

Your clients want the same.

3. Why Structure Builds Trust

A structured offer does one simple but powerful thing:

It shows that you've done this before.

It communicates:

Process

Experience

Focus

Clarity of thinking

People trust businesses that appeat to know what they're doing — and a well-packaged offer makes you look like you've already done the thinking for them.

Even if your service is tailored or flexible, you still need a shape:

Clear steps

Defined deliverables

Transparent timeframes

Thoughtful pricing logic

This is what builds perceived professionalism — and that's what wins clients.

4. The Three Elements of a Strong Package

There is no one size fits all template, but nearly all great packages answer these three questions

i. What's included?

Give the bones. The tangible stuff.
Help them picture the process and what they'll receive.
If possible, show stages or phases.

Example:

"Stage 1: Strategy session (60 min call)"
"Stage 2: Quote and outline with 3 options"
"Stage 3: On-site within 7 days of sign-off"

ii. What's the outcome?

This is what they're really buying — not the process, but the result.

Example:

"You'll have a clean, documented bid ready for submission — with no stress and no guesswork."
"You'll walk away with three ready-to-use proposals you can send immediately."

Make it real. Show the finish line.

iii. How does it work?

This answers logistical or emotional questions:
– How long will it take?
– What do I have to do?
– What if I'm not ready?
– How do I know this will work?

You're removing friction.

Example:

"We'll ask for 3 short calls, access to your existing quotes, and any testimonials you already have. We handle the rest."
"Need help with gathering information? We have a guided worksheet to make it painless."

5. The Danger of Loose Language

If your offer includes phrases like:

"Flexible packages available"

"Tailored to your needs"

"Bespoke services on request"

…you're likely creating confusion.

It sounds polite and accommodating.
But to the buyer, it creates more work:

"What do I actually get?"
"What's the price going to be?"
"How long will it take?"

The paradox is this:

The more flexible you sound, the less confident you seem.

Structure is not limitation — it's leadership.

6. Offer Design Principles

When designing your package, consider these proven tips:

 Give Options (But Not Too Many)

Three is the magic number.
i. Basic
ii. Better
iii. Best
Each one should make sense and include trade-offs.

This gives the client agency — without overwhelming them.

Anchor the Value

Start with the most complete offer — not the cheapest.
This sets the mental reference point.
Everything else then feels affordable by comparison.

Include Proof in the Package

Fold in results from past work:

"We've helped 24 business owners go from zero proposals to fully booked schedules — and this is the process we used."

Let the package carry the weight of your experience.

7. Examples of Better Packaging

Let's look at some weak vs strong examples:

"Consulting Day – $750"
"Growth Audit: One-day session to uncover where your message is losing sales, and how to fix it — with a 7-day action plan."

"Website Build"
"Three-page Conversion Site – includes copy, design, build, mobile-ready, and Google-indexed in 10 days."

"VA Services by the hour"
"10-Hour Monthly Package – for business owners who need help with inbox, scheduling, and customer follow-up — without hiring."

Can you feel the difference?

Each one takes a generic service…
…and turns it into a clear, valuable, confidence-building offer.

That's the power of packaging.

Exercise: Break Down Your Core Offer

Take your main service. Now break it into the 3 key components:

What's included?

List the steps, deliverables, or touchpoints.

What's the outcome?

Finish this sentence:

"At the end of this, the client will have…"

Or:

"The client will be able to…"

How does it work?

What does the client need to do?

How long does it take?

How do you make it easy?

Now take those answers and write a single paragraph that describes your offer.

Keep it simple. Then shape it into something someone could say yes to — without needing to ask, "So what do I actually get?"

8. What Changes When You Get This Right

When your package is strong, you stop chasing.

You don't have to defend your price — because it's clear what they're getting.
You don't get ghosted — because it's easy to say yes.

You don't get caught in endless tweaks — because the shape is fixed, and they know what to expect.

You become the person with a process.
The professional with a plan.
The one who makes things feel simple and safe.

This is how your offer becomes a solution, not a guess.

Where We Go From Here

Now that you've been seen the right way…
And your offer finally makes sense…

It's time to close the gap between interest and decision.

How do you ask?
What do you say to move from "thinking about it" to "let's go"?

That's the final piece of the 3 Ps — and it's one of the most important skills in business.

Let's move to:

Chapter 5: Propose — Ask Without Begging

Let's learn how to close without pressure — and turn clear offers into confident yeses.

PROPOSE

WIN APPROVAL

CHAPTER 5

Propose. You don't need to beg.

Most people ask for the sale too late, too weakly, or too vaguely. That's not confidence — its hesitation dressed up as politeness.

This Chapter will show you how to put together a strong, simple proposal that makes it easy for the client to say yes — and impossible to ignore.

How to present your offer in a way that earns trust, invites action, and closes the sale — without chasing

1. Why Most Offers Don't Convert

You've positioned yourself well.
You've packaged your offer clearly.

But the client still doesn't say yes.

Why?

Because you didn't propose anything.

You described.
You explained.
You sent a PDF.
You said, "Let me know what you think."

That's not a proposal.
That's a stall.

A proposal is a clear, confident invitation to take the next step — built around outcomes, trust, and action.

This Chapter is about writing and presenting that proposal in a way that gets chosen.

2. The Silent Signals You Send

How you propose tells the client how to respond.

If you sound unsure, they hesitate.

If you waffle or hedge, they overthink.

If you seem desperate, they distrust.

Here's the reality:

Every quote, email, or follow-up is sending a signal — even in silence.

Let's decode a few:

"Let me know what you think."
You're unsure. You've handed them the decision with no guidance.

"I can work around whatever suits you."
You've given up control and now sound like an order-taker.

"I hope that makes sense — happy to tweak if needed!"
You sound like you're seeking approval, not offering leadership.

These lines feel polite. They're trying to keep things "open."

But open loops don't close deals.

3. What a Proposal Really Needs to Do

A strong proposal does three things:

Restates the problem or need (so they feel understood)

Presents a clear path to the solution (so they trust your process)

Makes a confident ask (so they know what to do next)

Let's look at each.

4. Restate the Problem

Before you talk about what you offer, talk about why it matters.

"You mentioned that your biggest issue is getting bids submitted on time — and feeling like they actually reflect your business."

"Right now, your team is stretched thin, and you're not following up fast enough on leads — which means lost sales."

This proves you were listening.
It creates relevance and shows empathy.
It also sets up your solution — because now they want to hear it.

5. Present the Path

Now show what you're offering — and how it solves the problem.

This isn't just repeating the package.
This is tying it to their desired outcome.

"Here's what I recommend: a 3-step support package to help you win your next bid, without the stress. We'll handle the writing, manage the deadline, and submit on your behalf."

"You'll get:
– A focused 60-min strategy call
– A rewritten quote template that reflects your real value
– Three proposal rewrites to test with live leads"

"This means you'll feel more confident, close faster, and finally stop being ghosted after you send a price."

You're not just listing what you do.
You're showing how it helps.

6. Make the Ask

Now the part most people skip or soften:

Ask clearly. Ask confidently. Ask with a next step.

"If that sounds like what you need, I can start this week. Would you like me to send over the agreement?"

"Let me know if you'd like to book the first session, or if you'd prefer one of the other options."

"Would it help to get this started today?"

One of the most powerful versions of this comes from a spin on a technique from negotiation expert Chris Voss author of Never Split The Difference (a brilliant book by the way I urge you to read)

"Is there any reason we can't get started this week?"

That phrasing invites a no, which paradoxically unlocks the yes.

If they say "No, no reason," then you move forward.

If they say "Yes, there is…" — now you know the real objection.

Inviting a "no" gives them control — without losing yours.

7. Optional: Offer a Choice

Even better than asking for a yes is asking which yes.

Instead of saying, "Do you want to go ahead?"
Say:

"Would Option A or Option B be a better fit for you?"

Or:

"I've attached two versions — one with monthly support, one as a one-off. Which one feels more useful right now?"

This removes pressure.
It removes decision paralysis.
It lets the client feel like they're choosing how, not if.

8. The Problem with "Just a Quote"

Many clients will say, "Can you just send me a quote?"

Don't fall into the trap of emailing a number with no context.

A quote talks about price.
A proposal talks about outcomes.

You can still include the price — but surround it with meaning.

Tell them:

What they're getting

Why it matters

What will happen next

What results they can expect

This turns the quote from a cost into a decision that feels smart.

Even a short proposal email can do this.

9. Add Proof (Even Briefly)

Reinforce your proposal with one sentence of social proof.

"This is the same structure we used with ABC Ltd — they won their first two bids and now handle 3x the contract value."

"We used this process with 17 other cleaning businesses — 11 of them landed new commercial work within 30 days."

This doesn't have to be long.

Just enough to say:

You're not our first. You won't be our last. This works.

Exercise: Write a Simple Proposal Email

Choose a recent client you quoted (or could quote).

Now write a 3-part proposal email:

Restate their problem in one sentence

Present your offer and how it solves it

Make a confident ask

Use this structure:

Subject: Proposal — [Outcome-focused title]

Hi [Name],
Thanks for the chat earlier — I understand the main challenge is [problem].

Here's what I'd recommend:

[Clear offer — tied to outcome]
– [Deliverable 1]
– [Deliverable 2]
– [Deliverable 3]
This means [result/benefit].

Total cost: $[amount]
Start date: [day]
Next step: [action to confirm]

Would it help to get this started this week?

Best,
[You]

This email alone will outperform 90% of "just checking in" follow-ups.

10. What Changes When You Get This Right

When you learn how to propose — really propose — everything feels easier:

You stop chasing

You stop discounting

You stop wondering why people go quiet

Instead, you hear:

"Thanks — this is really clear."
"Yes, this feels like the right fit."
"We'd love to go ahead."

Not because you were clever.
But because you were clear, confident, and useful.

That's what wins.

Where We Go From Here

Now that you've learned how to be seen, how to make your offer make sense, and how to ask without begging…

…you might think we're done.

But now comes the engine behind all of it.

There's one simple phrase — and one powerful test — that pulls this all together and lifts your words from informative to irresistible.

You're about to meet it.

Chapter 6: The Engine — Which Means That and The So What Test

This is where your words go from good… to chosen.

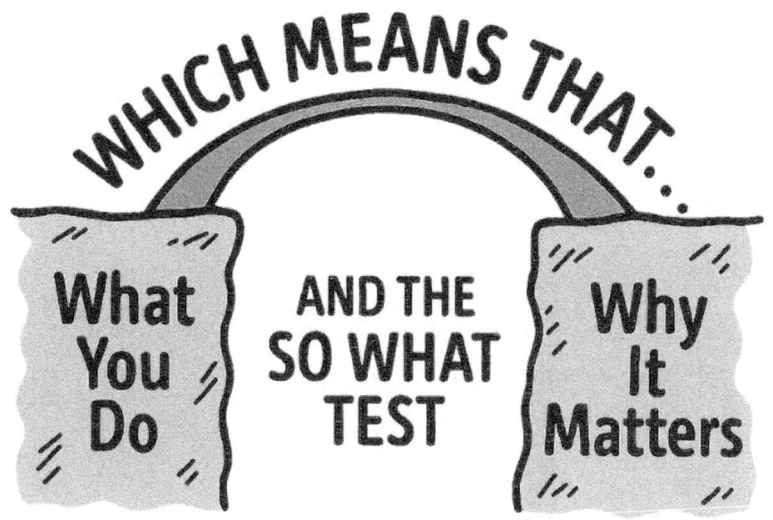

CHAPTER 6

This Chapter is the engine.

It's the most important tool in this book — and it's deceptively simple.

"Which means that…" turns vague claims into clear value. It's how you connect what you do to why it matters.

It's helped win $million's in business for my clients. And it's helped me win those clients in the first place.

You'll never look at your messaging the same way again.

The two most powerful tools in this book. Simple to learn. Impossible to unsee.

1. Why This Chapter Is Worth the Whole Book

If everything you've read so far has felt valuable, this Chapter is the multiplier.

You could take every other Chapter out and still walk away with something game-changing — if you just understand and apply what's inside this one.

That's not exaggeration. It's been proven in the field.

I've used "which means that" to help clients win $million's in paid work — across industries, sectors, and formats.

Not because it's clever.
But because it works.

Most messaging dies because it stops too early.

"We do X."

"We offer Y."

"We provide Z."

It's factual, but flat.
True, but forgettable.

And it leaves the reader — or listener — doing all the work.

"Which means that" is how we finish the job.

It's the bridge from what you do to why it matters.

It's the moment the penny drops.

It's the million-dollar moment.

2. The Real Problem with Most Business Language

Most people speak in bullet points and features.

They say:

"We do commercial cleaning."

"We offer a free consultation."

"We provide weekly reports."

"We've been in business for 20 years."

"We use eco-friendly products."

All technically true.

But none of it tells me why I should care.

That's because all those statements are about you.

They require me, the reader, to mentally translate that into benefit to me.

And if I don't have the time, energy, or understanding to do that?

I ignore you.

In messaging, the burden of translation is your enemy.

The client is already distracted. Already comparing. Already unsure.

Your job isn't just to tell them what you do.

Your job is to make them feel the benefit of it — instantly and clearly.

That's what "which means that" is for.

3. "Which Means That" — The Most Powerful Three Words in Business Writing

Let's say it again:

"Which means that..." is the most important phrase in this book.

Why?

Because it forces you to make your message relevant.

It forces you to finish the sentence.

It forces you to connect your input (the work you do) to the output (the value they get).

Here's the formula:

[What you do] + which means that + [Why it matters to them]

Examples:

"We include full onboarding and account setup — which means that you're ready to go from day one with zero tech stress."

"Our builders are all employed directly — which means that you get the same team throughout, and we never sub out your project."

"We use fixed-fee pricing — which means that there are no surprises, no 'extra' charges, and no awkward final invoices."

Each of those examples could have stopped at the first sentence.

But the second half is where the value is made visible.

It's where the penny drops.
It's where the client starts to nod.
It's where the decision becomes easier.

4. "Which Means That" vs Buzzwords

Compare these two versions:

"We offer a bespoke, flexible service."
"We tailor each job to your site and schedule — which means that we don't get in your way, and you're not paying for anything you don't need."

"We're committed to sustainability."
"We use only refillable cleaning products — which means that your building's carbon reporting just got easier."

"We pride ourselves on great customer service."
"We have a single named contact on every job — which means that you're never stuck in a call queue or repeating yourself to new people."

The second versions are better because they're clearer.

Not fancier. Not longer. Just clearer.

They show the real-world benefit of the claim.

And that's what makes people buy.

5. Different Ways to Say It (Without Losing the Power)

Let's be honest — if you write "which means that" in every paragraph, it can sound repetitive.

The idea is to use it often, but not always literally.

So here are some natural alternatives that do the same job — connecting your statement to a specific benefit.

So you can…

"We'll deliver a first draft in 48 hours — so you can meet your deadline without panic."

This helps you…

"We sort your evidence and testimonials — this helps you prove your value without chasing down old clients."

Which gives you…

"We quote fixed fees upfront — which gives you full cost certainty."

Resulting in…

"We work in pairs on-site — resulting in faster turnaround and less disruption."

Which lets you…

"We write your proposal and pricing narrative — which lets you stay focused on the day job."

That way…

"We handle compliance statements for you. That way, your bid ticks every box without needing legal input."

So, there's no…

"We send a written scope before work starts — so there's no confusion about what's included."

Use these to keep your writing varied — but don't stray too far. Clarity is king. Stick to simple connectors that force a benefit.

6. Case Study: How One Phrase Won the Work

A client of mine, a growing maintenance contractor, was bidding for a local authority contract.

Their draft response said:

"We have experience working in schools."

We applied "which means that" — and rewrote it as:

"We have experience working in schools — which means that our team are DBS-checked, trained to work around children, and used to operating discreetly during live term time."

That one line helped them stand out.
Because it wasn't just a claim — it was evidence of relevance.

That line got a full tick in the evaluation scoring system.
And the bid won.

7. The "So What?" Test — How to Catch Weak Messaging

Now we move from writing… to editing.

Because even great writers drift into vague, safe, padded statements.

The best way to fix this?

Ask "So what?" after every sentence.

It's brutal. But it works.

Try it:

"We've worked with dozens of clients across the sector."
– So what?
– "Which means that we know the likely pitfalls, delays, and expectations — and can pre-empt most issues."

"We offer flexible booking."
– So what?
– "Which means that you don't have to plan weeks in advance or fit around us."

"We've won multiple awards."
– So what?
– "Which means that others trust our work — and you're in good company."

If you can't answer "so what?" — the line shouldn't be there.

Or it needs rewriting.

This is the most powerful self-editing tool you will ever use.

Exercise: Power Up Your Messaging

Choose 5 sentences from your:

Website

Proposal template

LinkedIn profile

Pricing sheet

Sales email

Now for each sentence:

Ask "So what?"

Write a new version that answers it — using "which means that" or a variant.

For example:

Before: "We use high-quality, commercial-grade products."
After: "We use commercial-grade products — which means that your floors last longer, and you won't be calling us back for repairs in six months."

Do this once and you'll spot weak writing everywhere.
Do it regularly, and your words will start working harder than ever.

8. What You'll Start to Notice

Once you learn this technique, you'll see:

How many websites list tasks, not outcomes

How many quotes say what's included, but not why

How many proposals never connect the work to the client's world

How many testimonials are praise, not proof

And you'll start fixing them — fast.

You'll rewrite your own sentences on the fly.
You'll catch others drifting into padding.
You'll tighten your message until every line earns its place.

This is the moment your business starts sounding different — because it is.

9. What Changes When You Get This Right

When you use "which means that" and pass the So What Test:

You explain your value without jargon
You make your pricing easier to accept
You stop sounding like a generic provider
You start sounding like a solution
You make it easy to choose you

It's that simple — and that powerful.

This is the heart of the book.
Everything else builds around it.

Where We Go From Here

Now that you know how to make your words land,
you're ready to break through the noise.

Because even the clearest message needs attention first.

Next, we'll show you how to:

Stop sounding like everyone else

Catch the right people's attention

And make your first line earn the next one

That's what we cover in:

Chapter 7: Breaking Through the Noise

Let's make sure your million-dollar words get seen.

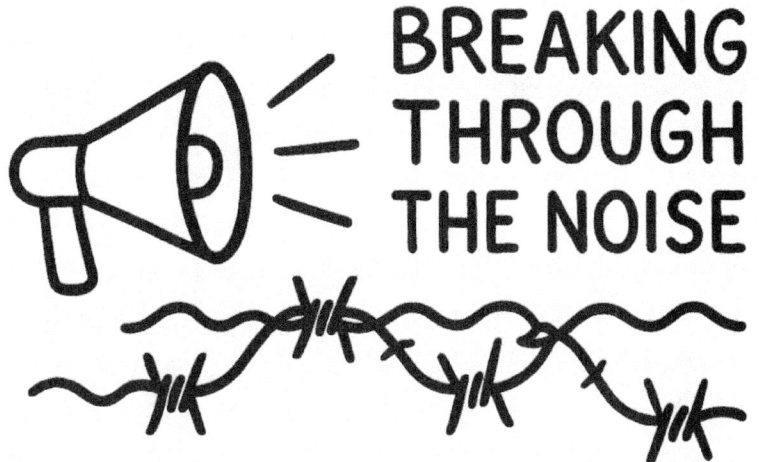

CHAPTER 7

How to get noticed in a crowded world without shouting, spamming, or sounding like everyone else

1. Attention Is Earned — Not Claimed

We live in a noisy world.

Everyone is "passionate."
Everyone is "committed to excellence."
Everyone offers "bespoke solutions tailored to your needs."

And none of that cuts through.

It's not because people are rude or dismissive.
It's because their brains are overloaded.

They're filtering everything:

- Emails
- Posts
- Sales pitches
- Quotes
- Flyers
- Adverts
- Conversations

Therefore, if your message sounds like everyone else… it will be treated like everyone else's — ignored.

And not because they didn't care.
Because they didn't even notice.

2. The Real Job of Your First Line

Your first line isn't to explain everything.
It's to earn the second line.

That's it.

Whether you're writing a proposal, a LinkedIn post, an email subject line, or even introducing yourself at an event — the first thing you say determines everything that follows.

Think of your message like a staircase.

Each sentence leads to the next.

But if the first step is slippery — they won't take it.

Your opening line is not where you convince.
It's where you catch attention by being specific, surprising, or useful.

Let's explore how.

3. Why Vague Openers Kill Interest

Here are common openers that kill attention:

"We're a forward-thinking business that…"
"Thanks for the opportunity to tender for…"
"At [Company], we pride ourselves on…"
"This proposal outlines how we aim to meet…"
"I just wanted to share…"

They're polite.
They're professional.
They're deadly.

They tell the reader:

"This is going to be like everything else."

And that's all the brain needs to move on.

4. What Strong Openers Sound Like

Here are better ways to begin — in all kinds of contexts.

Proposal:

"You want a contractor who finishes on time, without excuses — and who doesn't vanish when the job's done."

Email:

"Three reasons your current quotes aren't converting (and one easy fix)."

LinkedIn:

"Most cleaning companies say they're 'reliable.'
We prove it with a $50 if-we're-late guarantee."

About page:

"You've probably been burned before — late trades, hidden costs, no-shows. That's exactly why we built [Business Name]."

Each of these does one thing:

It starts in the client's world — not yours.

It hooks with something specific and emotionally relevant.

That's how you earn attention.

5. Behavioral Insight: Pattern Breaking

The human brain is brilliant at scanning.

It sees patterns in words — and skips what it thinks it's seen before.

This is why:

Most headlines get ignored

Most cold emails don't get opened

Most brochures get binned

Your job is not to shout louder.
It's to say something different enough to be noticed.

This is called pattern interruption.

It's why this line works better than a whole paragraph of praise:

"Here's how we get rid of the 'maybe next time' response in your quotes."

It breaks the reader out of autopilot — just long enough to care.

Once they care, you can do the real work.

6. How to Break the Pattern (Without Being a Gimmick)

You don't need to be shocking.
You don't need emojis.
You don't need to start every post with "Unpopular opinion…"

Here are three honest ways to break the noise:

Start with their frustration

"You're tired of being the cheapest quote — and still losing."

Start with a question they've asked themselves

"Ever wonder why your proposal gets viewed five times but never gets a reply?"

Start with a fact they don't expect

"Most tenders are lost in the first 150 words."

These aren't tricks.
They're relevant. They're real. And they work.

7. The Power of "Unsaid" Positioning

Sometimes, breaking through the noise isn't about what you say.

It's what you don't say.

Let's compare two approaches:

"We pride ourselves on customer service, quality workmanship, and integrity."
"We send a text before we arrive, show you what we did before we leave, and call back after 7 days to check everything's still perfect."

The second version never uses the words "customer service."

But it demonstrates it — clearly and memorably.

This is known as implicit positioning.

It's the most powerful way to be believed — because it never feels like selling.

8. How to Be the Most Interesting Business in the Room

Here's a secret:

You don't have to be interesting.
You must be interested.

If your message is built around them — their world, their goals, their problems — you will always sound sharper than competitors who talk about themselves.

Try this rewrite framework:

Before:

"We're an award-winning video agency based in the UK. We help clients stand out with innovative storytelling."

After:

"Most business videos are ignored after six seconds.
We help you get watched, remembered, and chosen — without scripts,
actors, or guesswork."

It's not louder.
It's clearer.
It speaks to a real concern.
And it gets noticed.

Exercise: Rewrite Your Opening Line

Pick one of the following:

Your LinkedIn headline

The first line of your homepage or About page

The first sentence in your proposals

Your intro when someone asks, "What do you do?"

Now rewrite it using one of these 3 openers:

Start with a frustration

Start with a specific result

Start with a bold, useful statement

Example:

Before: "We offer a range of cleaning services."
After: "We help landlords stop getting calls from tenants about the
same problems every week."

Keep it short.
Keep it true.
Make it feel real.

9. What Changes When You Get This Right

When you break through the noise:

Your emails get replies

Your posts get comments

Your proposals get read

Your intros get remembered

Your offer gets a second look — and a serious one

Not because you were louder.
Because you were clearer, sharper, and more useful.

And that's what people want.

They don't want to be pitched.

They want to be understood.

Where We Go From Here

You now have the engine.
You now have the attention.

But the next danger is this:

You weaken everything by using the wrong words.

It's not just what you say. It's how you say it — and too many people weaken their message without realizing.

So, in the next Chapter, we'll cut the softeners, qualifiers, and hedges.

We'll make your words stronger — sentence by sentence.

Chapter 8: Words That Weaken

Let's stop sounding unsure — and start speaking with power.

WORDS THAT WEAKEN

CHAPTER 8

How to spot and replace the silent saboteurs in your writing — so you sound confident, not cautious

1. The Words That Are Quietly Killing Your Message

You might be doing everything right.

Clear positioning

Smart packaging

A confident proposal

Specific outcomes

Clear benefits

But something still feels... soft.

You're not sure why — but your writing sounds hesitant.
Your message doesn't land with the strength you hoped.
Your pitch feels a little flat.

Often, the culprit isn't your structure.
It's your language.

Specifically, the little words that slip in and weaken your authority —
without you even noticing.

This Chapter is about removing them.

And replacing them with something stronger.

2. Weak Words: The Hidden Cost

Words that weaken your message do four things:

Undermine your authority

Dilute your value

Introduce doubt

Signal insecurity

They sound polite. Humble. Professional.

But they quietly tell your reader:

"I'm not sure."
"You might not trust me."
"Take this with a pinch of salt."

That's not confidence.
That's fragility.

Let's identify them — and then fix them.

3. The Top 10 Weakening Words and Phrases

i. "Just"

"I just wanted to check in…"
"Just a quick message…"
"We just help clients with…"

What it signals: You're apologizing for your presence.
Replace with: Nothing. Remove it. You don't need it.

ii. "Hopefully" / "I hope"

"Hopefully this helps."
"I hope that makes sense."

What it signals: You're unsure.
Replace with:

"Let me know if you need anything else."
"This should give you exactly what you need."

iii. "A little" / "Small" / "Quick"

"Just a small suggestion…"
"A quick favor…"
"We did a little work on…"

What it signals: You're downplaying effort or value.
Replace with:

"We've made a clear improvement."
"Here's an actionable suggestion."

iv. "I think…" / "It might be…"

"I think this could be helpful…"
"It might be a good idea to…"

What it signals: You lack conviction.
Replace with:

"This will help you…"
"A better approach is…"

v. "Obviously" / "Of course"

"Of course, this depends on…"
"Obviously, we'd tailor the package…"

What it signals: You're assuming — and subtly condescending.
Replace with:

"We tailor each package based on…"
Or simply cut the phrase.

vi. "If that makes sense"

"We'll start with a discovery call, if that makes sense."

What it signals: Uncertainty, or a fear of being challenged.
Replace with:

"We'll start with a discovery call — here's how it works."

vii. "Probably" / "Maybe" / "Kind of"

"It probably works best if…"
"We kind of specialize in…"

What it signals: Vagueness.
Replace with:

"This works best when…"
"We specialize in…"

viii. "Try"

"We'll try to get this to you by Monday."

What it signals: Lack of control or commitment.
Replace with:

"We'll deliver this by Monday."
Or if needed: "We aim to deliver this by Monday."

ix. "I'm not an expert, but…"

What it signals: You're undermining yourself — before you've even said anything.
Replace with: A well-framed insight.

"From what we've seen, clients in your position usually need…"

x. "In my opinion…"

What it signals: Your insights aren't solid.
Replace with: Authority.

"Based on what we've seen…"
"Here's what works best…"

4. Bonus: Overused Phrases That Sound Strong but Say Nothing

Some words don't weaken… but they waste space.

They sound big, impressive, or professional — but mean nothing.

Here are the worst offenders:

Innovative
Cutting-edge
Solutions-driven
Bespoke
End-to-end
Significant
World-class
State-of-the-art

These are not differentiators.
They're clichés.

Replace them with specifics.

"We offer innovative technology solutions."
"We build mobile apps that let your staff log reports instantly — even offline."

"We deliver world-class customer service."
"We answer 93% of calls in under 3 rings — and you'll always speak to the same person."

The difference?

The second version feels true.
Because it's measurable.
Concrete. Credible. Memorable.

Exercise: Strength Test

Pick a paragraph from:

Your website

Your proposal

Your LinkedIn bio

A sales email

Now go line by line:

Highlight all the hedges, softeners, or vague phrases

Rewrite them with stronger, clearer alternatives

Run each revised sentence through the "So what?" test

Example:

Original:

"We offer bespoke support packages tailored to your needs."

Rewritten:

"We offer three levels of support — so you only pay for what you need, and nothing you don't."

5. Behavioral Insight: We Trust Confident Language

People buy from people who seem certain — not loud, not arrogant, but confident.

Weakening language tells the brain:

"This person isn't sure. Maybe I shouldn't be either."

Strong language tells the brain:

"This person has done this before. I can trust this."

And the change is often tiny.

It's not about changing your personality.
It's about removing doubt from your words.

You're not making bigger promises.
You're making clearer ones.

6. What Happens When You Fix This

Your quotes stop sounding optional
Your proposals feel like safe decisions
You stop over-explaining
You get fewer "Can I think about it?" responses
You sound calm, experienced, and worth listening to

You also start trusting your own words.

And that's where confidence comes from.

Where We Go From Here

Now that you've stripped out the weak spots,
we're going to do the opposite.

We're going to find specific words and phrases that build trust — and explain why they work.

Because strong messaging doesn't just avoid mistakes.

It actively earns belief.

That's what's coming next:

Chapter 9: Words That Build Trust. Let's learn how to turn language into leadership.

WORDS THAT BUILD TRUST

CHAPTER 9

How to sound like someone worth listening to — without bragging, bluffing, or trying too hard

1. Trust Isn't Claimed. It's Earned Sentence by Sentence.

Here's something most people never think about:

Trust is being built — or broken — in every line you write.

Not just in your guarantees.
Not just in your testimonials.
Not just in your reviews.

In every word.
Every sentence.
Every quote.
Every email.
Every proposal.

So…

If people don't trust what you're saying, they won't trust what you're offering.

That's why this Chapter matters.

Because trust is what turns interest into action.
It's what closes deals.
And it's what stops people second-guessing after they say yes.

Let's learn how to build it deliberately.

2. What Trust Sounds Like

Trust doesn't sound big.
It doesn't sound flashy.
It doesn't sound like you're trying too hard.

Trust sounds like:

Calm
Precise
Confident
Measured

Specific
Honest

Here's an example:

"We're the best in the business."
"We've completed 42 similar jobs in the past two years — all signed off on the first inspection."

The second version is quiet.
It doesn't claim. It shows.

And showing is stronger than saying.

3. Specifics Build Trust. Vagueness Destroys It.

Let's look at some real examples:

Pricing page:

"Affordable packages to suit every need."
"Most clients invest between $750–$1,200 — all fixed price, no hourly rates, and no extras."

Proposal intro:

"We pride ourselves on delivering quality results."
"We're rated 4.9 stars on Trustpilot from 87 verified clients — and we guarantee a response within 4 working hours."

Cleaning company:

"We offer a bespoke service tailored to you."
"You'll have the same cleaner every visit — we never send strangers, and we text before we arrive."

The difference?

The second version feels true.

Because it includes:

Numbers

Timeframes

Tangible details

Sensory language

Process visibility

Those are the bricks that build trust.

4. The Power of Quiet Certainty

Some of the strongest phrases you can use are also the calmest.

Here are a few:

"Here's what to expect."
"This works best when…"
"You'll always speak to the same person."
"We've done this before."
"We don't do that — and here's why."
"We'll let you know if we're not the right fit."
"This may not be for everyone — and that's okay."
"Here's what we can't guarantee."
"We've built this based on what works in the real world."

Why are these powerful?

Because they signal:

Experience

Boundaries

Confidence

Clarity

Care

They're not loud.
They're certain.

And certainty builds trust faster than enthusiasm.

5. Don't Try to Impress — Be Useful

Trying to sound impressive often has the opposite effect.

Big words, vague claims, inflated titles, they trigger skepticism, not confidence.

Instead of trying to be the smartest person in the room…

Be the clearest person in the room.

That's who gets followed. That's who gets chosen.

Here's a good test:
Would a 12-year-old understand this?

If not, it's probably too complicated.

Trust isn't about sounding clever.
It's about sounding like someone who knows what they're doing —
and can explain it simply.

6. Borrowed Trust (And When to Use It)

You don't have to build all the trust yourself.
You can borrow it — ethically and effectively.

This is what social proof does.

But not all proof is equal.

Here are three forms of borrowed trust that work — and how to use them well:

i. Proof from others (Testimonials / Reviews)

"84% of our work comes from repeat clients."
"Here's what Jane, a property manager in Manchester, said after our first job…"
"We're rated Excellent on Trustpilot — based on 87 reviews."

Just make sure:

The quote is specific

The role of the reviewer is clear

The story supports the outcome you're offering

ii. Trust through place (Clients / Context / Geography)

"We've worked with three schools in this borough already — all still active clients."
"We operate solely in South Yorkshire — so we know the local compliance and suppliers."

This makes people feel like you're already relevant to their world.

iii. Process trust (How you work)

"Before we quote, we do a 30-minute walkthrough — so there are no surprises later."

"You'll always know what's happening — because we update every client every Friday."

Clear process = perceived professionalism.
And that earns trust.

Exercise: Build a Trust Box

Create a small collection of phrases or facts you can pull from in proposals, websites, emails, or intros.

Fill in each of these blanks:

"We've done this ____ times for clients like ____."

"You'll always ____."

"We don't ____ — and here's why."

"Most clients see ____ within ____."

"This works best when ____."

"You'll speak to ____, not ____."

"The last time we did this, ____ happened."

Once written, these become your trust triggers.
Use them everywhere your business shows up.

7. A Note on Honesty

The fastest way to build trust?

Tell the truth. Especially when others don't.

Be honest about timelines

Be clear about pricing

Say when something isn't guaranteed

Admit what's not included

Acknowledge what's not in your control

This kind of clarity isn't weakness. It's strength.

Buyers remember the one who told them the truth — even when it wasn't convenient.

Because that's who they feel safest saying yes to.

8. What Happens When You Do This Right

When you use words that build trust:

Your proposals get accepted faster
You get fewer "what if" questions
You stop having to "sell" — because they already believe you
You reduce price resistance
You stop chasing and start being chosen

And you start to feel more certain in your own voice.

Because your words don't need to sell.
They just need to be believable.

Where We Go From Here

You've now got the strength.
You've got the clarity.
And you've got the trust.

But there's one more trap to avoid:

Padding. Overexplaining. Rambling.

Because sometimes, we write more than we need to — and say less than we think.

So next, we strip everything down.

We get lean. Sharp. Effective.

Chapter 10: Redundant Words and Bloated Phrases

Let's make every word work harder.

REDUNDANT WORDS AND BLOATED PHRASES

CHAPTER 10

How to strip the padding from your message — and say more by writing less

1. When Clarity Becomes Clutter

You've worked hard to sound clear.
To show your value.

To build trust.
To get attention.

But there's one more enemy of clarity — and it often shows up last:

Too many words.

This is what happens when:

You keep explaining after the point has landed

You repeat yourself without adding new value

You add qualifiers to make things "sound better"

You say something twice, in slightly different ways

You use three words when one would do

It's not fatal.

But it's friction.

Every unnecessary word adds a second of hesitation.
Every bloated phrase makes your reader work harder than they should.

And in a world where people are already scanning, not reading — that hesitation is where attention dies.

This Chapter is about removing that friction.

2. How to Spot Redundancy in Your Writing

You'll usually find it in these places:

In your opening paragraphs

In list items that say the same thing in multiple ways

In long sentences with filler clauses

In phrases you've copied from other proposals

In jargon you don't need, but feel like you "should" include

The good news?

You don't need to guess.

You can spot redundancy with two tools:

The Highlighter Test

The Echo Test

Let's look at both.

3. The Highlighter Test

Print out your message. Get two highlighters.

Use one to highlight anything that adds value — clear benefits, outcomes, strong proof.

Use the other to highlight anything that's just "holding space."

You'll often find entire sentences that can be cut without losing anything.

Here's an example:

"We've taken the time to carefully consider all aspects of this project and look forward to potentially working together on this opportunity."

That sounds polite. But what does it add?

"We've reviewed the brief and are ready to deliver on time and within budget."

Same intent.
Half the words.
Twice the clarity.

4. The Echo Test

Redundancy often hides in repetition — saying the same thing twice in different words.

Examples:

"We provide honest, transparent, and trustworthy service."
Choose one of those words — and show it with evidence.

"We are committed to excellence and strive to achieve high standards."
Just say:

"We deliver work that passes inspection first time — or we fix it at no cost."

When you spot the echo, trim it.
You'll find your message feels stronger — not shorter.

5. The Most Common Redundant Phrases (and What to Use Instead)

Bloated phrases are like packing material in a shipping box. They make the thing look bigger, but they add no real value — and they slow down the delivery.

Trim them out and your message lands faster, cleaner, and with more impact.

Here's your starter list. Use it. Then watch for your own patterns —
because every writer has a few pet phrases that creep in.

Bloated Phrase	Better Alternative	Why It Works
At this moment in time	Now / Currently	Removes four wasted words.
Due to the fact that	Because	Shorter and more natural.
In order to	To	Cuts clutter without losing meaning.
A large number of	Many	More concise and conversational.
In the event that	If	Direct and easy to process.
Has the ability to	Can	Simpler and more confident.
Make contact with	Contact	Avoids unnecessary filler.
End result	Result	"End" is implied.
Absolutely essential	Essential	"Absolutely" adds nothing.
Future plans	Plans	All plans are about the future.
Added bonus	Bonus	"Added" is redundant.
Close proximity	Near / Close	"Proximity" already means near.
Completely unanimous	Unanimous	"Completely" is implied.
Whether or not	Whether	"Or not" is built in.

Bloated Phrase	Better Alternative	Why It Works
Advance warning	Warning	All warnings are given in advance.
Past history	History	"Past" is redundant.
Basic fundamentals	Fundamentals	"Basic" is implied.
True fact	Fact	All facts are true by definition.
End conclusion	Conclusion	"End" is implied.
Collaborate together	Collaborate	Collaboration already means "together."
At all times	Always	Simpler and more direct.
Completely destroy	Destroy	"Completely" is implied.
Return back	Return	"Back" is implied.
Refer back	Refer	Same as above — "back" adds nothing.

How to Use This List

1. **Run a "search" in your document** — check for these phrases before you hit send.

2. **Replace or cut** — don't just swap words, also see if you can tighten the sentence further.

3. **Watch your own habits** — keep a running note of bloated phrases you tend to use.

Mini Exercise — Spot & Trim

Take a recent email, proposal, or LinkedIn post.
Highlight every word or phrase that could be shorter without changing the meaning.
Replace them.
Read the new version out loud — notice how it moves faster and hits harder.

6. Case Study: Quote Trimmed, Win Secured

A client sent over a 3-page quote for review.

The first paragraph alone said:

"Thank you very much for the opportunity to submit this proposal. We've taken the time to review the tender specification in full, and we are confident that we are in a strong position to deliver this work to the highest standard of quality and professionalism."

It's polite.
But it's saying nothing the buyer doesn't already know or needs to hear.

We rewrote it to:

"We're ready to deliver — and we meet every requirement in the spec. Here's how."

No filler.
No preamble.
Straight to the point.

The buyer called it "the clearest bid we've seen."

They won.

7. Being Clear ≠ Being Cold

Now a quick warning:

Cutting words doesn't mean cutting warmth.

You're not becoming robotic.
You're becoming readable.

You can still sound human:

"Thanks again for the opportunity. We're excited to help you deliver this project."
"Let's keep this simple — here's what we suggest."

Be warm.
Be kind.
But don't waste people's time.

They'll appreciate it more than you think.

8. Bonus: The $1,000 Test

Here's a favorite mental trick:

Pretend every word you write costs $1,000.

Would you still write:

"We strive to deliver an unparalleled level of excellence across all aspects of our business..."?

Or would you say:

"We deliver good work, fast — and fix it if you're not happy"?

Shorter. Cheaper. Stronger.

Exercise: The Word Clean-Up

Choose a page of writing — a proposal, homepage, quote, or intro.

Now:

Highlight every phrase that sounds long, formal, or generic

Replace it with something clearer and shorter

Ask yourself: does this still say the same thing — faster?

Set a goal: reduce the word count by at least 25% without losing meaning.

You'll find that:

Shorter often means stronger

Clearer means more confident

The final message feels more professional — not less

9. What Happens When You Trim the Fat

People read more
Your key messages stand out
You get fewer follow-up questions
Your pricing makes more sense
You sound like someone who respects the client's time

You also feel lighter.

Because your writing becomes easier to write — and easier to say.

And that's the goal.

Not to write more.
But to say more — with less.

Where We Go From Here

Now that your message is lean, let's shift focus.

Because clarity alone isn't enough.
Context matters.

The next Chapter is about how you frame what you say — because even the right words can fall flat if they're framed the wrong way.

Next up:

Chapter 11: The Power of Framing

Let's learn how to shape your message so it lands harder — without changing the facts.

THE POWER OF FRAMING

CHAPTER 11

Why how you say it changes everything — even when what you say stays the same

1. The Frame Is the Message

Imagine two signs on two identical food stalls:

"10% chance of food poisoning."
"90% chance of no issues."

Same product.
Same math.

Different frame.
Which one do you walk toward?

Framing is how you shape a message before it lands.
And the frame is often more powerful than the message itself.

People don't hear your words in a vacuum.
They hear them through context, emotion, and expectation.

Get the frame right, and your message becomes magnetic.
Get it wrong, and even your best work can go unnoticed.

Let's learn how to frame like a pro.

2. You Already Use Frames — You Just Don't See Them

Framing happens in everyday life:

Saying "invest" instead of "cost"

Calling it a "bonus" instead of an "extra"

Saying "you'll save 3 hours" instead of "it takes 1 hour less"

These are frames — subtle shifts that change how your offer is perceived.

In business writing, framing is everywhere:

- In how you describe your services
- In how you handle objections
- In how you present your price
- In how you introduce your team
- In how you compare options

When used well, it changes the whole game.

3. The Three Core Framing Tools

Let's break it down into three powerful, practical tools you can use immediately.

i. Reversal Framing — Turn a weakness into a strength.

You take something that might sound like a downside, and you reframe it as a deliberate choice.

Example:

"We're a small team."
"We're deliberately small — so our clients always work directly with us, not a junior."

"We don't offer 24/7 support."
"We keep regular hours — which means we're fresh, focused, and not juggling shift rotas when working on your job."

Use reversal framing when:

You need to address an objection

You want to make a limitation feel like a benefit

You're doing something differently — on purpose

ii. Comparison Framing — Shape how people see the price, time, or result.

You're not just giving information — you're anchoring it to something familiar.

Example:

"This package costs less than one month of missed rent on a single property."
"It's about the same as a boiler service — but it protects you from $5,000 in fines."

This works because:
People don't always know if your price is high or low.
They only know how it feels — and comparisons guide that feeling.

Use comparison framing when:

Quoting a price

Asking for time

Describing a return

Positioning urgency

iii. Outcome Framing — Move from features to results.

This is the heart of Million Dollar Words — and where "which means that..." lives.

You don't just say what you do — you show why it matters.

Example:

"Includes a full compliance check."
"Includes a full compliance check — which means you won't get caught out at inspection."

"We'll contact tenants directly."
"We'll contact tenants directly — which means no extra admin for you."

Outcome framing is about drawing the line between what you do and what they get.

When in doubt, ask:

"So what?"

If you can't answer that clearly, the message is incomplete.

4. Real-World Framing in Action

Let's compare a before and after:

BEFORE (Generic proposal):

"Our team has extensive experience in property maintenance, and we take pride in delivering high-quality work to our clients."

AFTER (Framed proposal):

"We've been handling commercial property maintenance for 15+ years — which means faster fixes, fewer call-backs, and peace of mind that you're legally covered."

What changed?

The vague term "experience" became specific (15+ years)

The pride claim was dropped

The outcomes were made visible

The language moved from internal ("we take pride") to external ("you're legally covered")

That's framing in action.

5. Framing and Pricing

Want to reduce price objections?
Don't change the price — change the frame.

Here's how:

Frame around waste:

"That leak is adding $60 a month to your bill — this fix pays for itself in 10 weeks."

Frame around regret:

"Most people only call us after something goes wrong — we'd rather help before that."

Frame around time:

"This will save your team 10 hours a month — every month."

Frame around safety:

"Non-compliance fines can hit $5,000+. This protects you against that."

Remember:
People don't mind paying for value.
But they hate paying for nothing.

Framing shows them what they're really buying.

6. Use Their World as the Frame

The most powerful framing?
Use what they already care about.

"This helps you stay under budget — without cutting corners."

"You'll reduce complaints from tenants — especially in older buildings."

"This stops your inbox filling up with avoidable problems."

This works because it:

Speaks their language

Enters their world

Frames your service through their lens

And when you frame through their priorities, it feels like you understand them.

Which means they're far more likely to say yes.

Exercise: Reframe Your Offer

Take one of your core messages — something you say often. Now reframe it in three ways:

Reversal frame: Turn a perceived weakness into a strength

Comparison frame: Compare it to something familiar

Outcome frame: Show what it means to the buyer

Example:

Original:

"We don't offer a same-day callout."

Reversal: "We plan all work in advance — so nothing gets rushed or missed."

Comparison: "Our response time is faster than most emergency callouts — without the panic pricing."

Outcome: "You'll always know when we're coming — and we'll stick to it."

7. What Happens When You Frame Well

Your offer feels more valuable — without changing the price
You address objections before they're raised
You sound more confident
You connect with what buyers actually care about
You position yourself as the obvious, safe, smart choice

And none of it requires lying, exaggerating, or overselling.

You just put the right frame around the right truth — and let it land.

Where We Go From Here

Framing gives your message shape.
Now it's time to give it empathy.

Because if you want to be listened to — not just heard — you need to show people that you get it.

Empathy in Language

CHAPTER

How understanding your audience changes everything about how you write and speak

1. Why Empathy Matters More Than Ever

In a world full of noise, the most powerful thing you can do is show your audience that you truly understand them. Empathy is about stepping into their shoes, seeing the world through their eyes, and addressing their needs, fears, and desires.

Empathy in language is not about sympathy or simply being nice, it's about making your audience feel seen and heard, which builds trust and connection. Let's dive into how you can weave empathy into your messaging.

2. Listen First, Write Second

Empathy starts with listening. Before you write a single word, you need to understand your audience's world. What are their biggest challenges? What keeps them up at night? What are their goals and dreams? The more you listen, the better you can reflect their reality in your writing.

Practical Tip: Spend time in the spaces where your audience hangs out—forums, social media groups, industry events. Take note of the words they use and the issues they discuss. This will help you speak their language.

3. Reflect Their Reality

Empathy means showing your audience that you understand what they're going through. Use their pain points and aspirations in your messaging.

Example:
Instead of saying, "We offer top-notch cleaning services," try, "We know how frustrating it is to deal with inconsistent cleaning—our team ensures your space is spotless every time, so you never have to worry."

This approach shows that you get their pain and are there to solve it.

4. Use "You" More Than "We"

A simple but powerful way to infuse empathy into your writing is to focus on the reader. Use "you" more than "we" to keep the focus on their needs, not just your services.

Example:
Instead of saying, "We provide excellent customer service," say, "You'll always get a response within an hour because your time matters."

This subtle shift makes your reader the hero of the story.

5. Acknowledge Their Concerns

Empathy means not shying away from the fears or concerns your audience might have. Address them head-on and show them that you understand.

Example:
"You might be worried about hidden costs. We get it. That's why we provide a detailed breakdown upfront, so you know exactly what to expect."

By acknowledging their concerns, you build credibility and trust.

6. Show That You're on Their Side

Empathy means positioning yourself as a partner, not just a provider. Make it clear that you're invested in their success.

Example 1
"We're here to make sure you get the best results possible"

Empathy means positioning yourself as a partner, not just a provider. Make it clear that you're invested in their success and that you genuinely care about their outcomes.

Example 2
"We're here to make sure you get the best results possible." When you succeed, we succeed. Consider us an extension of your team, always looking out for your best interests."

This kind of language reassures your audience that you're not just there for the transaction but for the long haul.

7. Use Simple Examples to Create Connection

Instead of detailed stories, you can use brief, simple examples that mirror your audience's experiences. This helps create that sense of empathy without diving into lengthy narratives.

Example:
"Think of how frustrating it is when a maintenance issue goes unresolved for weeks. We ensure that doesn't happen by responding within 24 hours."

This kind of example quickly shows you understand their pain point and have a solution.

8. Speak Their Language

Empathy also means using the same language and terminology your audience uses. Reflecting their words back to them makes your message feel more relatable and tailored to their needs.

Example:
"If your audience frequently talks about 'tenant satisfaction,' use that

exact phrase in your messaging rather than substituting it with something like 'customer happiness.' It shows that you understand their priorities and are paying attention to what matters to them."

9. End with a Reassuring Tone

Empathy is also about leaving your audience feeling understood and reassured. End your messages on a note that reinforces your commitment to their success and well-being.

Example:
"Rest assured, we're here to support you every step of the way. Your success is our priority, and we won't rest until you're completely satisfied."

This helps build a lasting relationship based on trust and understanding.

Where We Go From Here

Now that we've covered how empathy can transform your language and help you connect deeply with your audience, it's time to take that understanding and apply it across all your communication channels. Empathy isn't just a tool for one-on-one interactions; it's the foundation for building a loyal and engaged audience.

In the next Chapter, we'll dive into how to transform information into insight, ensuring that every piece of communication you share is meaningful and impactful.

From Information to Insight

CHAPTER 13

How to ensure every piece of communication delivers real value

1. Why Insight Matters More Than Information

In today's world, information is everywhere. What people truly crave is insight — those nuggets of wisdom that help them see things differently, make better decisions, or understand a problem more clearly.

Turning information into insight is what sets great communicators apart. It's the difference between sounding helpful… and being remembered.

Let's make sure every message you send delivers more than just data. Let's make it valuable.

2. Connect the Dots for Your Audience

Insight often comes from connecting the dots your audience hasn't connected yet.

That means taking facts, features, or results — and drawing out the deeper meaning.

Example:
"This software update reduces processing time."
"This update will save you 10 hours a week — time you can now reinvest into growing your business."

Same input. But the second version feels valuable.
That's insight.

3. Ask "So What?" to Find the Insight

When you're unsure if something adds value, ask the same question we've used before:

"So what?"

It's a ruthless but powerful way to turn flat information into something meaningful.

Example:
"Our service is available 24/7."
"So you can get help any time — even at 3am — and avoid costly delays."

Keep going until you find the answer that matters.

4. Frame Information Around Outcomes

Outcomes stick. Processes don't.

Always tie what you do to what it means.

"We use the latest cleaning technology."
"Which means your property stays spotless longer — with fewer call-backs and lower costs."

Don't leave your audience to figure out the benefit.
Show them.

5. Use Analogies to Simplify Complex Ideas

A good analogy makes you sound smart without sounding complicated.

"Our onboarding system automates multi-channel integration workflows."
"It's like switching from a paper map to a GPS — you'll get where you're going, faster, with fewer wrong turns."

Analogies make complex ideas click. Use them generously, especially when describing unfamiliar tools or processes.

6. Highlight the "Why" Behind the "What"

Your audience doesn't need to know everything you do.
They need to know why it matters.

Example:
"We conduct monthly site audits."
"To catch small issues early — before they become big, expensive ones."

Facts are useful.
But the reason is what gets remembered — and acted on.

7. Use Data to Tell a Story

Don't just drop numbers. Wrap them in meaning.

"Clients saw a 30% reduction in downtime."
"Which means fewer interruptions, more productivity, and a better bottom line — all within 3 months."

Numbers are credible. But stories are memorable.
Combine both, and you build trust and interest.

8. Make Insights Actionable

A great insight is something your audience can use — not just something they nod at.

"Knowing that preventative maintenance reduces emergency repairs by 50%, schedule your next check this week."

Don't stop at "here's what we know."
Add: "Here's what you can do next."

9. Personalize Insights for Relevance

Generic advice is easy to ignore.

Tailor insights to your reader's situation, language, and priorities.

"Our tools improve team productivity."
"For property managers like you, that means fewer follow-ups, faster tenant response times, and fewer missed inspections."

The more specific you are, the more valuable you become.

10. Reinforce Insights with Proof

The most powerful insights are backed by experience or evidence.

"This pricing approach helped a local contractor double conversion rates — without reducing fees. It works because it makes the value feel clearer from the start."

You're not showing off.
You're showing that you've seen this work — and it can work for them too.

11. Encourage Reflection and Dialogue

When insight lands, it often triggers a pause — a moment of thought.

You can make that moment more powerful by inviting reflection:

"What would change if you made this shift today?"
"Which of your current proposals could be improved with this approach?"

This isn't about teaching.
It's about sparking something useful.

Where We Go From Here

You now know how to turn raw facts into messages that land — and stick.

That means you can:

Make your proposals more persuasive
Make your emails more actionable
Make your conversations more useful
Make your website more memorable

You're no longer just informing.
You're helping people see.

But there's one more skill that lifts everything you've learned so far:

The ability to guide someone — with your words — toward the right decision, without pushing, bragging, or begging.

That's what we explore next.

Language That Leads —
Guiding Without Pushing

CHAPTER 14

How to shape decisions through your words — without sounding pushy, vague, or unsure

1. You're Not Trying to Convince. You're Trying to Guide.

If you've made it this far, you already know the value of being clear, relevant, and outcome focused.

But now we take things further — from understood to acted on.

Because great messaging doesn't just explain.

It leads.

It nudges the reader in the right direction.
It makes decisions easier, not harder.
It gives them a path — not pressure.

This Chapter is about writing like someone who knows what they're doing...
...and helps the client feel that they know what to do next.

2. Why Most Messages Feel Weak

Let's look at how most people end an email, a proposal, or a pitch:

"Let me know what you think."
"I'm happy to help if needed."
"Just wanted to see if this sounds okay?"

They're polite.
They're safe.
But they don't lead anywhere.

They leave the decision hanging in mid-air — like a balloon with no string.

That's not helpful. That's hesitation.

Instead, your job is to lead without pushing.
To make it easier to say yes than to stall.

3. Leadership Language vs Permission-Seeking Language

Let's make this practical.

Here's the difference:

Permission-Seeking Language	Leadership Language
Would you like me to…?	Here's what we'll do next…
If it's okay with you, I could…	I'll arrange for this to be done…
Do you want me to send the details?	I'll send the details over today…
Is it alright if I…?	I'll get started on this now…
Let me know if you're happy for me to…	I recommend we move ahead with…
Would you mind if I…?	I'll take care of that for you…

The second column isn't pushy. It's calm, clear, and professional.

It shows direction — not desperation.

4. Friction Lives in Uncertainty

When your language leaves too many open questions, the client feels the weight of decision-making.

"Do I need to compare this to others?"
"What happens if I say yes?"
"What exactly am I agreeing to?"

That's friction. And friction leads to silence.

Great messaging removes friction by doing the following:

Sets expectations
Confirms the next step
Gives the reader confidence that they're being looked after

You're not forcing a decision.
You're reducing doubt.

5. Use Certainty Without Arrogance

The most trusted voices don't shout.
They speak plainly — and with calm certainty.

Here are some examples:

"Here's how this usually works."
"This structure works best when…"
"Let's start with the first call — I'll send the link now."
"We've done this before. You'll be in good hands."
"Nothing starts until you're fully happy with it — and I'll walk you through each part."

This isn't fake confidence.
It's clear, grounded language that shows you're not winging it — and they won't have to either.

6. Give Fewer Choices, Not More

You don't need to list every possible option.
You need to guide people toward what makes sense.

"Most clients choose Option B — but A and C are there if needed."
"If you're unsure, we'll start with X. You can always upgrade later."
"This one gets you moving fastest — we can refine as we go."

This does two things:

It builds momentum.

It removes overwhelm.

Leading means giving shape to the decision — not opening every possible door.

7. Offer "Next Steps" That Feel Natural

Don't leave people hanging.

Even if you're not "closing a deal," your message should still point somewhere.

Here's what that can sound like:

"If it's a yes, just reply with 'Let's go' and I'll take care of the rest."
"If you'd like to explore this, book a quick call here: [link]"
"If now's not the right time, just let me know — no hard feelings."
"If you've got questions, send them through — I'll answer anything."

This is soft leadership. You're not pushing.
You're inviting a next step — and making it easy.

8. Write Like the Outcome Already Makes Sense

Here's a small but powerful shift:

Start writing as if the decision to go ahead is already reasonable.

"When we start, I'll walk you through…"
"The first step is booking your intro call here."
"Once this is confirmed, you'll receive [X]."

This language doesn't assume the sale.
It prepares for it — and makes the outcome feel expected.

The reader doesn't feel sold to.
They feel supported.

9. Bonus: The "Is There Any Reason..." Technique

Again we refer Bck to negotiation expert Chris Voss, this is one of the most powerful leadership lines in business:

"Is there any reason we couldn't start this next week?"

It invites a no — which either confirms a yes or surfaces the objection.

It keeps you in control, builds safety, and still leads the conversation forward.

It's counter intuitive I know but it works. Try it!

It's about showing that you're ready if they are — and if they're not, you can deal with that too.

Exercise: Rewrite Your Final Paragraph

Grab the last paragraph from:

a proposal, a pricing email, a pitch message or your website's contact page...

Now check:

Does it end on "let me know," "happy to help," or "get in touch"?
Or does it say: "Here's the next step — and here's why it makes sense"?

Rewrite the ending using one of these leadership closers:

"Here's how to move forward..."

"If this sounds good, I'll send the agreement today."

"Next step is [action] — unless you have any final questions."

"Would it help to get this in place by [date]?"

Use language that leads. Calmly. Clearly. Without pushing.

10. What Changes When You Get This Right

You sound like a pro — not a vendor
You stop chasing — because next steps are built in
You reduce ghosting — because people know what to do
You get chosen faster — because decisions feel easy
You feel more confident — because your message is in control

It's not about pressure.
It's about posture.

When you lead with your words, people follow with their yes.

Where We Go From Here

Now that you know how to lead with calm, confident language…

It's time to stack your toolkit.

There are phrases — short, punchy, practical ones — that move conversations forward, win attention, and build belief.

We call them:

Million Dollar Phrases.

They're coming next.. Let's build your shortlist.

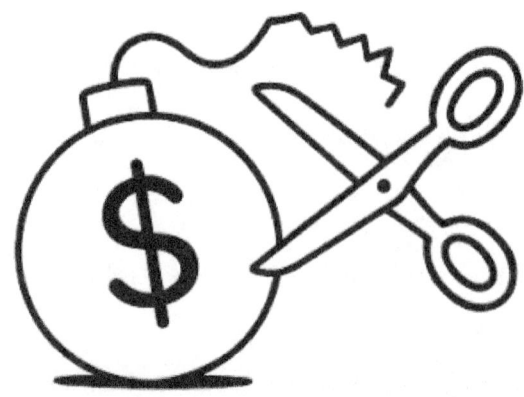

Million Dollar Phrases — Shortcuts to Yes

CHAPTER 15

Simple phrases that make your message land harder, faster, and more clearly

1. What Makes a Phrase "Million Dollar"?

Some phrases work harder than others.

They cut through confusion.
They calm doubts.

They move people forward — without needing paragraphs of explanation.

You've already met the king of them all:

"Which means that…"

But this Chapter expands your collection.

We're going to build a shortlist of powerful, practical phrases that earn trust, guide decisions, and make it easy to say yes.

You don't need fancy words.
You need the right words — at the right moment.

2. The 7 Roles of a Million Dollar Phrase

Every great phrase in this Chapter does one or more of the following:

- Makes the benefit obvious
- Reduces perceived risk
- Builds trust or credibility
- Invites a next step
- Gives clarity without needing a full pitch
- Frames the decision positively
- Replaces weak words with something useful

If a phrase doesn't move the needle — it doesn't belong here.

3. The Core Collection

Here are 12 proven, high-impact phrases — each with its purpose, example, and variation.

i. "Which means that…"

Translates features into benefits.

"We deliver in 48 hours — which means that your team won't be waiting around."

Variations:
– "So you can…"
– "This gives you…"
– "That way…"

This is your go-to phrase. Use it everywhere — but vary the form when needed.

ii. "Most people choose…"

Reduces decision anxiety by offering a default.

"Most people choose Option B — it includes everything you need; without extras you won't use."

It creates safety by showing what others do.
(Especially helpful when offering multiple packages.)

iii. "If it helps…"

Offers support without pressure.

"If it helps, I can send over a quick outline for you to review."

It softens the lead, while still guiding action.
A gentle phrase that opens the door without sounding salesy.

iv. "Would it help if…?"

Moves the conversation forward with calm leadership.

"Would it help if I put together a draft for you to review this week?"

This is a question with intent. It invites action but gives control.

v. "You're not the only one…"

Normalizes hesitation and builds trust.

"You're not the only one who's found proposals tricky — that's exactly why I built this system."

This phrase reassures. It says: You're not wrong. You're just not supported — yet.

vi. "We've done this before."

Builds credibility without bragging.

"We've done this before — same challenge, same pressure, same deadline."

Used sparingly, this line delivers authority in a single sentence.

vii. "Here's what usually works best."

Adds structure and guidance without sounding bossy.

"Here's what usually works best — we start with a 45-minute call to map everything out."

This gives your offer shape and direction — and people like being led when it feels safe.

viii. "Here's how to move forward."

Provides clarity at the exact moment people stall.

"Here's how to move forward: pick a slot that works, and I'll take care of the rest."

It removes ambiguity. It tells people what to do and makes that action feel easy.

ix. "Nothing starts until you're ready."

Reduces risk and builds safety.

"Nothing starts until you're ready — and I'll walk you through the whole process."

It tells the client they're in control — but also that you're prepared and ready to go.

x. "Let's keep this simple."

Cuts complexity. Signals confidence.

"Let's keep this simple — here's what I recommend."

It gives the reader permission to stop overthinking. You're taking the wheel (lightly).

xi. "There are no surprises."

Builds trust and removes doubt.

"There are no surprises — everything is fixed price, and you'll know what's coming at each step."

Used well, this phrase pre-empts fear.
It's powerful in pricing, scope, and delivery.

xii. "This might not be for you — and that's okay."

Disarms resistance and positions you with strength.

"This might not be for you — and that's okay. But if it is, it'll work exactly the way I've outlined."

Paradoxically, this builds desire.
It says: This works. I'm not desperate. The choice is yours.

4. What These Phrases All Have in Common

They don't try to impress.
They don't overcomplicate.
They don't talk about features or irrelevant details.

They do one thing:

They make action feel easy and smart.

And that's the job of every line in your message.

You're not writing to be remembered.
You're writing to be chosen.

Exercise: Phrase Swap

Take one of your current messages — a proposal, a quote, a sales page, or an email.

Now look for these weak or vague phrases:

"Let me know what you think"

"We're proud to offer…"

"Please don't hesitate to…"

"We'd love the opportunity to…"

"Here are our services…"

Now replace them with Million Dollar Phrases like:

"Here's how to move forward…"

"Most people choose…"

"This might not be for you — and that's okay."

"Let's keep this simple…"

"Nothing starts until you're ready…"

Do a full rewrite using just 2–3 strong phrases.

You'll instantly feel the difference.

5. What Happens When You Use These Well

Your message gets read to the end
Your proposals land stronger
You reduce ghosting and hesitation
You sound like someone with a process
You get chosen faster — and with fewer questions

Million-dollar phrases don't sell for you.
They remove resistance.

That's what great messaging does — one sentence at a time.

Where We Go From Here

You've now got the structure, the clarity, and the phrases that lead people to yes.

But what happens when that yes gets stuck behind doubt?

Next up:

Chapter 16 - Objections. Delays. Resistance. Silence.

In the next Chapter, we'll cover how to handle them — with confidence and calm.

CHAPTER 16

What to say when people hesitate, stall, or resist — and how to turn doubt into progress

1. Objections Aren't the End - They're a Signal

Let's get one thing straight:

Objections aren't a rejection.
They're a request for clarity.

They mean:

"I don't feel ready yet."
"Something here doesn't make sense."
"I need help deciding."

And if you've done everything right so far — positioned clearly, packaged sensibly, and proposed confidently — most objections will be simple to handle.

This Chapter gives you the language to do exactly that.

Without pressure.
Without panic.
Without playing games.

2. Most Objections Aren't Really About Price

People say it's about price.
It rarely is.

It's about uncertainty. About risk. About trust.

So, before you reach for a discount, reach for better language:

Reassure
Realign
Redirect

Your words need to say:

"I hear you. That's a fair concern. Here's what that means — and what we'll do next."

3. Three Types of Objections (and What They Really Mean)

Stalling ("Let me think about it...")

They're unsure what to compare this to or what happens next.

Instead of chasing, try:

"No problem — just so I don't clog your inbox, is there anything that feels unclear or off right now?"

You're giving them space — but staying present.

Price ("It's too expensive...")

They're not yet convinced of the outcome or value.

Instead of defending, try:

"Totally fair — and I never want to push something that isn't right. Is it the total cost, or something else that's causing concern?"

Or:

"Just to be clear, the goal here isn't to be the cheapest — it's to deliver [outcome]. Would it help to revisit how that looks for your situation?"

Don't justify the number.
Clarify the return.

Timing ("Not right now...")

They believe the problem exists — but not urgently.

Instead of pushing, try:

"Understood. Out of curiosity — what would need to happen for this to feel more urgent or useful?"

Or:

"I totally get that. But just so I know, is this a 'later' or a polite 'no'?"

Gentle. Direct. No drama.

4. Use Reassuring Phrases That Keep the Door Open

Here are some you can use almost anywhere:

"If now's not the right time, that's okay — but I'll leave this here in case it helps down the line."

"You're not alone — most clients had the same concern before we started."

"There's no pressure at all — I'd rather we both feel it's the right fit first."

"I don't want you to guess. Let's walk through the parts that matter most to you."

These phrases do one powerful thing:

They remove pressure while still holding attention.

5. Pre-Empt Objections With Clarity

Most objections are preventable.

Build your messaging to answer them before they arise:

Clearly explain pricing and what's included

Confirm next steps in plain English

Include FAQs or "What happens if…" answers

Tell them what others asked before saying yes

This doesn't make you pushy.
It makes you prepared.

6. Use the "Is There Any Reason..." Close

You've seen this earlier — now let's go deeper.

"Is there any reason we couldn't get this started next week?"
"Is there anything holding this back from being a yes?"

This technique:

Makes it easy to say "no" to obstacles

Encourages honesty

Gives you the real reason they're hesitating

It's calm. Controlled. Respectful.

And it puts you in a position to solve the real issue.

7. When to Walk Away (With Confidence)

Not every lead will land. Not every no becomes a yes.

That's okay.

Sometimes the most powerful phrase you can use is:

"Sounds like this isn't the right fit — and that's fine. If things change, I'll still be here."

This does two things:

Preserves your posture

Leaves the door open

You're not needy.
You're professional. And you've got standards.

Exercise: Objection Rehearsal

Pick a service or offer you currently sell.
Now answer these four prompts:

What are the top 3 objections you hear most often?

What's really behind each one? (Uncertainty? Budget? Timing?)

How can you reassure and redirect — without pushing?

Write one calm, confident sentence for each objection using the formats above.

Then save those responses and use them in:

Your proposals

Your emails

Your follow-ups

Your FAQs

Objection handling isn't just about closing.
It's about clarity — and trust.

8. What Happens When You Do This Well

You stay in control without being pushy
You reduce awkward silences and ghosting
You earn respect — even when they say no
You start hearing more "yes" responses — sooner
You build confidence in your own process

Objections aren't signs of failure.
They're invitations to step up and lead.

Where We Go From Here

You now have the tools to lead through hesitation.

But what if the hesitation is yours?

What if you're still not sure how to speak with confidence on paper —
especially when you're new, self-taught, or still building?

That's where we go next.

Confidence on Paper – When You're Unsure

CHAPTER 17

How to sound like a pro, even when you don't feel like one yet

1. Confidence Comes From Clarity, Not Credentials

Let's say this up front:

You don't need years of experience, fancy logos, or industry awards to write with confidence.

You just need to be:

Clear on what you offer

Sure of what it helps people do

Willing to say it plainly and without apology

Confidence on paper doesn't mean pretending.
It means owning what you know — and saying it in a way others can believe.

This Chapter helps you do that, even if you're still figuring things out.

2. What Insecurity Looks Like in Writing

You've seen it (maybe even written it):

"I'm still learning, but I hope this helps…"

"I'd love to be considered…"

"Sorry if this isn't quite what you had in mind…"

"Let me know if you think I'm a good fit?"

This language doesn't build bridges.
It builds doubt.

The reader doesn't know if you're capable — because you're not acting like you are.

Here's the shift:
You don't need to fake confidence.
You need to remove hesitation.

3. Own What You Do Know

You may not know everything. That's fine.

But you know something. And someone out there needs that.

Instead of apologizing for what you lack, lead with what you deliver:

"This is a simple, proven approach that gets results — and it's built to get you moving fast."

Or:

"This won't solve everything — but it will get you past the current block and save time in the process."

Confidence is honest.
That's why it works.

4. Use Clear, Certain Language (Even If You're Nervous)

Confidence doesn't mean chest-thumping or overclaiming.
It's about removing doubt from your words — so the other person feels steady in your hands.

Examples are on the next page.

These lines aren't arrogant.
They're calm and competent.
You can drop them into proposals, emails, presentations, or conversations.

Phrase	When to Use It	Why It Works
"Here's what will happen next."	Setting out a process or next steps.	Shows control and makes the path clear.
"We can deliver that by [date]."	Confirming timelines.	Replaces vagueness with certainty.
"The best way forward is…"	Guiding a decision.	Positions you as a trusted advisor, not a passenger.
"This approach will…"	Presenting your solution.	Speaks with assurance instead of hedging.
"That's included."	Answering scope/coverage questions.	Simple, positive, and eliminates doubt.
"Here's what we'll do."	Explaining actions.	Active voice puts you in the driver's seat.
"We've done this before for [client/sector]."	Offering proof.	Normalizes success — no hype, just precedent.
"This will take [X time] and achieve [Y result]."	Linking timeframe to outcomes.	Connects efficiency and value.
"We recommend…"	Making a choice on the client's behalf.	Saves them decision fatigue and shows expertise.
"That's already in place."	Addressing concerns about readiness.	Removes a worry instantly.

Phrase	When to Use It	Why It Works
"I'll confirm that for you today."	Handling uncertainty.	Promises swift closure without overcommitting.
"We've accounted for that."	Responding to potential obstacles.	Shows foresight and preparation.

5. Set Boundaries, Not Apologies

You don't need to be available 24/7.
You don't need to say yes to everything.
And you don't need to shrink your language to keep people happy.

Here's how boundaries sound confident, not cold:

"To do this properly, I'll need a decision by [X]."
"This process works best when we stick to [Y timeline]."
"We're a good fit if you're looking for [Z] — and happy to refer you elsewhere if not."

This is what pros sound like.
Clear. Focused. Not desperate.

6. Let Simplicity Do the Heavy Lifting

Complicated language often hides a lack of confidence.

People over-explain, hedge, or pad their writing to "sound smart."

But great messaging sounds like this:

"Here's what I recommend. It's simple, it works, and you won't waste time."

That line works — whether you're brand new or ten years in.

Why?
Because it sounds useful.

And useful beats impressive, every time.

7. Borrow Strength from Systems and Process

If you feel unsure, lean on your system — even if it's simple.

"Here's the 3-step plan I use to [solve the problem]. We'll walk through it together."
"Every client starts with a short call. It helps shape everything we do next."
"I've built a checklist, so nothing gets missed — it's simple but powerful."

You don't need to impress.
You need to show you've thought it through.

Confidence lives in structure — not sparkle.

8. Show What You Stand For

One of the best ways to sound confident is to stop trying to sound neutral.

Take a stand on something that matters to your client.

"I don't believe in jargon-filled proposals. I believe in clarity that helps you win the work."
"We don't do 30-page presentations. We fix problems, fast — and keep you in the loop."

"This isn't about selling you more. It's about helping you move forward."

Even if you're new, this kind of conviction commands respect.

Exercise: Rewrite One Message Without Hedging

Take one message you've sent recently — a proposal, pitch, or email where you didn't feel 100% confident.

Now scan it for weak phrases like:

"I think..."

"Hopefully..."

"Let me know..."

"Sorry if..."

"Just checking in..."

Rewrite it using language from this Chapter.

Focus on:

What you know

What you deliver

What happens next

Why it helps

Read it out loud.
Feel the difference in tone, posture, and energy.

That's confidence — even if your hands are still shaking.

9. What Happens When You Get This Right

You stop sounding like you're asking for permission
You get chosen — even if you're not the biggest or most established
You feel more in control, because your words reflect your value
Clients trust you faster
You stop apologizing for where you are — and start showing up as who you are

You don't need to be loud.
You don't need to be slick.
You just need to be clear, steady, and useful.

That's what people buy.

Where We Go From Here

You're sounding more confident. You're removing resistance. You're guiding decisions.

Now let's bring in one of your biggest secret weapons:

Other people's words.

But not just any testimonials.

We're going to show you how to ask for, shape, and use testimonials that help you win work.

Better Testimonials –
How to Ask and
What to Use

CHAPTER 18

Because "They were great!" doesn't move the needle

1. Testimonials Are Proof, Not Praise

Most testimonials don't help.

They say things like:

"Really nice to work with."

"Great service!"

"Would definitely recommend."

It's all positive — but it's also vague, generic, and forgettable.

And worst of all?

It doesn't help the next client say yes.

This Chapter will fix that.

Because a great testimonial doesn't just say you're good...

It says:

"This worked for me — and here's how."

That's when testimonials become tools — not just thank-yous.

2. What a Great Testimonial Actually Does

It gives your next client:

Confidence you can deliver
A sense of what the result looks like
A picture of what working with you feels like
Relief that someone like them already said yes — and was glad they did

It turns abstract promises into real-world proof.

It moves you from potential to proven.

3. Why Most Testimonials Fall Flat

Here's why most testimonials don't help:

They're too short ("Fantastic.")

They're too generic ("Did a great job.")

They don't say what actually happened

They don't say who the client is or what they needed

They sound written to please, not to persuade

So your job isn't just to collect testimonials.

It's to shape better ones.

4. The STAR+D Format

Here's how you do it — use a simple structure:

Situation — What was the client dealing with?
Task — What did they need from you?
Action — What did you actually do?
Result — What changed for them?
+Demonstration — What does that show others?

Here's an example:

"We were struggling to win tenders — getting shortlisted but never landing the work. We needed help turning our technical language into something that connected with buyers. Alan took our last three submissions and restructured them completely. The next bid scored 94%, and we won it. That win changed everything — it showed us we could compete at this level."

It's specific.
It's relevant.
It's believable.

That's a Million Dollar Testimonial.

5. How to Ask for a Testimonial (Without Feeling Awkward)

Here's a simple line you can use in an email, DM, or conversation:

"Would you be open to writing a short line or two about your experience working together? Something that shows what you were looking for — and what changed?"

Or even:

"Quick favor — could you describe what was going on before we worked together, and what shifted as a result? Even a short note would be gold."

You're not asking for praise.

You're asking for a before-and-after story.

And people are usually happy to help — especially if you made their life easier.

6. What If They Struggle to Write It?

Offer to write a draft for them to approve.
That's not unethical — it's helpful.

Most clients are happy for you to make their words sharper, as long as they're true.

Here's a message you can send:

"Totally fine if writing's not your thing — I can draft something based on our project, and you can tweak or approve it."

Now you're saving them time — and you're in control of the quality.

7. Where to Use Your Best Testimonials

Don't just stick them in a "Reviews" tab.

Put them next to the offer they relate to.

On your sales page
In your proposals
In your quotes
In emails
In social posts
Anywhere you want a buyer to say "yes"

Treat testimonials like proof points — not decoration.

8. Add Details

Here's how to add punch to a testimonial:

Include the client's name and role (with permission)
Add numbers or timeframes
Mention specific wins or avoided problems
Use their own language where possible

Example:

"We were about to spend $8,000 on a new website. Alan helped us clarify the message first — and we realized we didn't need a new site, just a clearer offer. That saved us a fortune, and we're now booking more calls than ever."

It's short — but full of story.

Exercise: Testimonial Toolkit

Think of three clients you've helped, even small wins.

For each one, write down:

What was going wrong before?

What did they need from you?

What did you do?

What changed afterward?

Draft a testimonial using the STAR+D structure.

Send it to them with this message:

"I pulled together a short summary of our work together. Would you be happy to use this as your testimonial? Happy to edit if needed!"

This turns vague reviews into powerful proof.

9. What Happens When You Get This Right

You build credibility without bragging
You remove doubt before it has a chance to grow
You sound proven — not just promising
You get chosen faster, especially by risk-averse buyers
You create a story others want to step into

People trust people.

When they hear that someone like them got a result from someone like you they're far more likely choose to do business with you.

Where We Go From Here

Testimonials help back up your offer.

But they only work if the rest of your message gets read in the first place.

And that's where we go next.

Let's make your writing easier to scan, easier to follow, and harder to ignore.

Writing for the Scanner—Formatting for Attention

CHAPTER 19

Because if they don't read it, it doesn't matter how good it is

1. Most People Don't Read — They Scan

Let's be honest:

People are busy.
They skim.

They scroll.
They glance.

And that means even your best ideas can be missed — unless your writing is built to catch eyes, hold attention, and guide the reader through.

This Chapter shows you exactly how.

Because formatting isn't decoration.

It's strategy.

2. Use Headings to Break the Flow

Before — Wall of Text:
We can complete the work in two weeks, including all preparatory steps, quality checks, and handover. This will allow your team to start using the system immediately after delivery and take advantage of the seasonal uptick in sales.

After — Scanner-Friendly:

Timeline

- **Two weeks** from start to completion.

What it means for you:

- Immediate go-live.

- Capture seasonal sales peak.

Why it works:
Headings stop the scroll. They give the eye an anchor, and the brain a label for what's coming.

3. Short Paragraphs Win

Before:
The training package covers system navigation, troubleshooting, and best practices. It will be delivered over three half-day sessions to minimise disruption. Each session will be recorded for your reference. We've run this programme for over 50 teams.

After:

Training Package
We'll cover:

- System navigation.

- Troubleshooting.

- Best practices.

Format:

- 3 x half-day sessions.

- All recorded for your reference.

- Proven with 50+ teams.

Why it works:
Short paragraphs and bullet lists make it impossible to miss the essentials — even in a quick skim.

4. Bullets for Proof

Before:
We have extensive experience in this area, including work for leading clients in your industry. Our solutions have helped clients improve efficiency by an average of 20%, cut costs by 15%, and boost satisfaction scores by 25%.

After:

Proven Impact:

- **20%** efficiency gain.

- **15%** cost reduction.

- **+25%** satisfaction.

Why it works:
Bullets break out facts so they land instantly. Numbers in bold stick in the mind.

5. Use Numbered Lists for Process

Before:
To get started, we first scope the requirements, then prepare the documentation, and finally launch the system once testing is complete.

After:

How We Work:

1. Scope requirements.

2. Prepare documentation.

3. Test and launch.

Why it works:
Numbered lists show sequence. They make it easy to follow the order — and see the end point.

6. Bold for Benefits

Before:
We'll complete the audit in five days. This means you'll have clear, actionable steps to improve before the next inspection.

After:
We'll complete the audit in **five days** — giving you **clear, actionable steps** to improve before your next inspection.

Why it works:
Bold highlights benefits mid-sentence without breaking the flow. The eye can't help but land there.

7. White Space is Your Friend

Before:
We recommend starting in September so the changes are in place for your busiest quarter. This will help you capitalise on peak demand and avoid the December bottleneck when suppliers slow down.

After:

Start in **September**
→ Changes in place for your busiest quarter.
→ Avoid the December supplier bottleneck.

Why it works:
White space isn't empty. It gives breathing room so each line hits harder.

8. Use Boxes, Quotes, or Pullouts to Highlight Gold

Before:
If we start next week, the project will be completed in ten days, which means you can take advantage of the summer demand and secure additional revenue before the end of the quarter.

After:

Start next week → live in 10 days.
That means you can capture summer demand and boost revenue before quarter-end.

Why it works:
It interrupts the visual rhythm. They spotlight the one line you most want remembered.

9. Structure Your Message Like a (short!) Story

Even a pricing page or proposal should feel like it flows:

Problem

Solution

Proof

Next step

Use formatting to guide the reader through that arc.

Headings introduce
Bullets simplify
Bold and spacing create momentum
Final line shows what happens next

Every section should answer:

"Why should I keep reading?"

Exercise: The 3-Minute Scan Test

Take one of your recent proposals, quotes, or emails.

Step 1: Set a timer for 3 minutes
Step 2: Print or open the message
Step 3: Glance — don't read every word
Step 4: Ask yourself:

What jumped out?

What got skipped?

What felt heavy or cluttered?

Could someone get the gist without reading everything?

Now revise the layout using:

Spacing
Headings
Bullets
Bold

Make it scannable — and your message gets seen.

10. What Happens When You Get This Right

People read what you send
You sound professional before they read a word
Decisions get made faster
Less back-and-forth, more "Let's do it"
You stand out in a sea of lazy layouts

You've already got the right words.
Now you've got the right format to deliver them.

Where We Go From Here

You've written something worth reading.

But how do you know it's working?

How do you make it sharper, clearer, and more effective — without second-guessing every line?

That's what's next.

The Re-Read Test – Making Your Message Worth a Second Look

CHAPTER 20

Because great messaging doesn't just get read — it gets remembered

1. The First Read is for Attention. The Second is for Action.

Let's start with something most people overlook:

If your message doesn't hold up on the second read, it probably won't lead to action.

Anyone can get a glance.
But if someone goes back, scans it again, and still feels clear and confident?

That's when they move.

This Chapter gives you a simple test to make sure your message is doing its job — not just filling space.

2. Why Messages Get Skipped, Ignored, or Forgotten

It's rarely because of the product or offer.

It's because the message:

- Was too long
- Tried to sound clever instead of being clear
- Said everything… and nothing
- Didn't land the value
- Had no momentum — no next step

The solution?
Apply the Re-Read Test before anything goes out the door.

3. The Re-Read Test — 5 Quick Questions

Before you send anything important — email, proposal, landing page, pitch — ask:

If I skimmed this, what would I remember?
–If the answer is "not much," something's wrong with the formatting or message weight.

Where does my eye land first — and is that the right thing?
– Make sure the scannable parts (headings, bold, bullets) reflect the value, not the admin.

Does every section lead to the next?
– Look for dead zones. Anything that feels like a detour or repetition needs cutting.

Is it clear what action to take?
– If the reader has to scroll back to figure out what to do, you've lost momentum.

Would I feel confident saying yes after reading this?
– That's the million-dollar question.

If it doesn't pass these five, revise before sending.

4. Trim Anything That Doesn't Earn Its Place

You're not writing to impress.
You're writing to move someone forward.

Look for:

Padded intros

Repeated points

Empty statements ("We're committed to quality...")

Overexplaining what's already clear

Long blocks of text hiding one small idea

Ask:

"If I deleted this, would the message be sharper?"

If yes — delete.

5. Repeat the Core Message (But Not the Same Way)

Repetition can be powerful — if it reinforces the right thing. (which you must have noticed in the book your reading right now!)

Example:

"This gives you faster results.

It's designed to save you time and deliver outcomes within weeks — not months.

That's why most clients say it pays for itself in the first month."

Same message. Three different angles.

This isn't padding.
This is reinforcement.

6. Read It Out Loud (Seriously)

It's a cliché for a reason:

What sounds clunky out loud will feel clunky on the page.

When you read it out loud, you'll catch:

Sentences that run on

Phrases that don't land

Awkward transitions

Jargon you didn't realize was there

If you stumble, pause, or wince — fix it.

Out loud is your quality control.

7. Check the Ratio of "You" vs "We"

One of the fastest ways to make your message more powerful?

Count the "you"s vs the "we"s.

- "You get…"
- "You'll be able to…"
- "You can finally stop…"

vs.

- "We offer…"
- "We believe…"
- "We're proud to…"

If your message is about you, they'll lose interest.

Shift the lens. Make it about them.

Exercise: Take the Test

Grab a message you've sent recently — proposal, quote, page, or post.

Now answer:

What line would I remember if I only skimmed this?

Is that the most important part?

Do the bold bits and headings guide me through the message?

Do I know exactly what the message wants me to do?

Is this something I'd say, out loud, to a real client?

Revise until the answer to all five is YES.

This is how good messages become great.

8. What Happens When You Do This Well

People get the point — faster
You sound sharper, clearer, more professional
You get replies like "This makes total sense — let's go"
You spend less time following up and chasing
You win more work with less effort

The re-read test doesn't take long.
But it leaves a lasting impression.

Where We Go From Here

You now know how to write messages that hold up to scrutiny.

But here's the final piece of the puzzle:

Making sure those messages sound like you.

In the next Chapter, we focus on voice — how to sound natural, confident, and consistent across every message you write.

The Voice of You – Owning Your Tone and Style

CHAPTER 21

How to sound like yourself… at your most clear, confident, and compelling

1. Your Voice Is Your Advantage

There's no shortage of polished, professional content out there.

And most of it sounds… the same.

If you recall in the introduction to this book I made it clear this wasn't a book to help you find your voice – more to use the voice you already have and ensure it comes through in how you communicate – for clarity, unambiguity, authority and to ensure you don't sound like everyone else…

"We're passionate about delivering innovative solutions."
"Our mission is to provide world-class service."
"We strive for excellence in everything we do."

It's bland.
It's corporate.
And it could be written by anyone.

But your real edge?

You sound like a human.

And if you sound like yourself — clear, honest, grounded — people will feel like they already know you.

That's trust.
That's influence.
That's what gets remembered.

There a many great books on this subject so this chapter is not meant to be a substitute for them, instead its just a nudge towards how to sound authentically you and why.

2. What Is a "Voice," Really?

Your voice is the tone, rhythm, and personality your writing carries.

It's not about being quirky or funny (unless that's you).

It's about consistency and clarity — showing up the same way, every time.

It's how people recognize you in a crowd of sameness.

3. The 4 Ingredients of a Strong Voice

Every distinct voice includes four key elements:

    i.   Tone – Friendly? Direct? Professional? Irreverent?
    ii.   Pace – Short punchy lines? Long flowing sentences? A mix?
    iii.   Language – Plain English? Industry terms? Humor? Formality?
    iv.   Values – What do you stand for? What don't you tolerate?

When you write in your voice, all four are working together.

Example:
"This might not be for you — and that's okay. But if it is, it'll work exactly how we've described. No drama, no nonsense."

That sentence says: calm, confident, clear boundaries.

That's a voice.

4. Don't Imitate — Anchor

It's tempting to imitate others:

A trendy founder's casual tweets

A big brand's quirky tone

A "smart" industry style full of jargon

But imitation makes you invisible.

Instead, anchor your voice in how you already talk when you're at your best - calm, clear, useful.

Write like the version of you that people trust in conversation.

5. Speak It Before You Write It

A simple trick:

Say what you want to write out loud — then write that down.

It'll be shorter.
More direct.
Less padded.

Example:

"Our objective is to deliver end-to-end visibility across all workflows."

"We help you see what's going on — and what's getting in the way."

Which one sounds like a person?

6. The 3-Lens Check

When refining your voice, check every sentence through these three lenses:

Would I say this out loud?

Would my ideal client understand this instantly?

Does this sound like me — or like a brochure?

If the answer to any is no — rewrite it.

7. Make It Easy to Trust You

The right voice builds trust by doing this:

Removes ego
Avoids jargon
Uses simple, strong phrases
Makes promises that feel doable
Says "I don't know" when needed
Sounds consistent across every message

Consistency beats cleverness.

If your voice is clear and steady, people will believe the message —
even if they're hearing it for the first time.

8. Include Your Edges (Yes, Really)

Voice isn't just about smoothness. It's also about edges.

That might be:

A touch of wit

A directness others avoid

A way of simplifying things others overcomplicate

A stance on what matters and what doesn't

Example:

"I don't do 50-page decks or waffle-filled proposals. I do simple, clear
messaging that wins work."

That's voice. It might not suit everyone. But it will attract the right
ones.

Exercise: Define Your Voice

Use this quick framework to shape your voice:

I want to sound…
(Choose 3–5 words)
→ e.g. calm, clear, honest, confident, no-nonsense

I want my readers to feel…
(What emotional tone should land?)
→ e.g. supported, informed, reassured, energized

Things I will always say…
(E.g. short sentences, outcomes over features)

Things I will never say…
(Jargon, hype, empty adjectives, apologies)

Now go back to a recent message and rewrite it using this lens.

9. What Happens When You Get This Right

People feel like they know you
You attract better-fit clients
You stop overthinking — and write faster
Your message gets clearer, punchier, more believable
You sound like a pro, without trying to "sound professional"

This isn't about branding.

It's about being recognizable, real, and consistent — in every message you send.

Where We Go From Here

You've now found your voice.
You've sharpened your structure.
You've written to lead, not just to inform.

So what happens when the stakes go up?

Big pitch. Big opportunity. Big moment.

Let's build your response for that moment — the kind of proposal that wins work.

Million Dollar Proposals – How to Win with Words

CHAPTER 22

Turning ideas into action and quotes into contracts

1. A Proposal Isn't a Quote — It's a Decision Tool

Let's kill this myth now:

A quote gives a price. A proposal makes a case.

One shows what it costs.
The other shows why it's worth it.

Million Dollar Proposals don't just say what you'll do.
They say why it matters, how it helps, and what happens next.

They're short, sharp, and full of confidence — not just numbers and niceties.

And if you get them right, they'll win you more work than any pitch ever could.

2. What a Winning Proposal Really Does

It gives the client:

- A clear understanding of what's on offer
- Proof that you understand their needs
- A sense of how working with you feels
- Confidence in the outcomes
- A simple next step

In short — it removes doubt and replaces it with certainty.

Because people don't buy when they're convinced — they buy when they feel safe.

3. The 5-Part Million Dollar Proposal Structure

Here's your simple, proven layout:

i. Introduction — Show you've listened

A short paragraph that says, "We get it."
Example:
"You mentioned [problem], and the goal is to [outcome]. This proposal sets out how we'll make that happen — clearly, quickly, and with no surprises."

ii. What You'll Get — Keep it clear

A bullet list or short section outlining the service, deliverables, or scope.
Stick to results and clarity. Avoid jargon.

iii. Why This Works — Build belief

A paragraph or two explaining how this solves the problem, framed in their world.
This is where you use "which means that" and make your offer land hard.

iv. The Investment — Frame the value

Show the pricing with confidence. Add context if needed.
Example:
"The investment is $2,400 — fixed. This covers the entire process from planning to handover. No add-ons. No surprises."

v. Next Steps — Make it easy to say yes

Explain exactly what happens next.
Example:
"If this looks good, just reply 'Let's go' and we'll send the agreement. Once signed, we'll get started this week."

Optional: Include a testimonial, short case study, or visual element that reinforces credibility.

4. Proposal or Email? Use Both.

Don't hide your proposal behind a vague message like:

"Please see attached…"

Instead, write the proposal email as the pitch, and the attached PDF as the backup.

Let your email summarize:

- The problem
- The offer
- The price
- The next step

If they don't open the attachment, they should still be able to say yes.

5. Use Formatting That Builds Confidence

Use the same formatting principles we covered earlier:

- Short paragraphs
- Bold for key lines
- Headings as signposts
- Bullets for clarity
- Plain, confident language

The reader should feel smart — not overwhelmed.

Make saying yes the easiest part of their day.

6. Pre-Handle Objections Inside the Proposal

Don't wait for the "but…"

Tackle it up front:

Worried about the timeline?

"This process is fast — we'll have the first draft in 5 days."

Concerned about value?

"This pays for itself within weeks — most clients recover the cost in the first month."

Nervous about commitment?

"You can pause or adjust at any point — it's flexible by design."

Great proposals calm the brain and make the heart nod along.

7. What About Proposals for Bigger Projects?

Longer doesn't mean better.

For larger proposals, add:

A project timeline

A breakdown of milestones

A short bio or track record

Optional extras (clearly marked)

Terms — but written in human English where possible

Still keep the tone: direct, steady, human.

The goal is the same — make it feel safe to say yes.

8. The "Million Dollar" Line to Include

Here's a sentence to adapt and use in nearly every proposal:

"This is designed to solve [X], so you can [Y] — and we'll walk you through every step."

It proves three things:

1. You understand the problem.

2. You've built the solution deliberately.

3. You'll guide them through it.

That line alone has won more contracts than most people's 30-page decks.

Variations You Can Use:

i. **Outcome First:**
   "We'll get you from [current state] to [desired state] — and we'll guide you through it from day one."

ii. **Problem + Certainty:**
   "We've built this to remove [pain point] so you can [result] — and we'll be with you at every step."

iii. **Short & Punchy:**
   "Solves [X]. Gets you [Y]. We'll handle the how."

iv. **Process Confidence:**
"This tackles [X] head-on, delivers [Y], and we'll lead you through the process without the guesswork."

v. **Collaborative:**
"We'll work with you to solve [X] so you can [Y] — with full support from start to finish."

Tip:
Write yours in under 20 words.
Lead with the client's problem and outcome, not your process or features.
Make "we'll walk you through every step" — or its equivalent — the reassuring close.

Exercise: Build Your Core Proposal Template

Open a blank doc

Create these headings:

What You Said

What You'll Get

Why This Works

Investment

Next Steps

Under each, write 2–3 sentences you'd be happy to reuse or adapt for future clients.

Save it as your Million Dollar Proposal template — and refine it as you go.

This will save you hours — and help you win more work with less guesswork.

9. What Happens When You Do This Right

Clients feel understood
You sound confident, not desperate
You get chosen faster — with fewer questions
You stop sending "quotes" and start sending clarity
You win more work, more often — even against bigger competitors

Proposals aren't admin.
They're sales tools.

Use them like you mean it.

Where We Go From Here

You've now built a powerful proposal engine.

But proposals are just one part of the bigger picture.

Next, we'll zoom out — and look at the ecosystem of messages that win business.

From quick messages…
To lead magnets…
To full-on campaigns…

Let's build a messaging system that works — even when you're not online.

The Message Ecosystem — Multiply Your Impact

CHAPTER 23

How to turn one clear message into a hundred opportunities

1. Great Messaging Doesn't Live in Isolation

You've written the proposal.
You've nailed the offer.
You've tightened up the words.

But if those words only exist in one place — you're underusing them.

Million Dollar Words don't just help you win the work. They help you attract, convert, and retain that work, too.

This Chapter is about making your message work harder — across every part of your business.

2. What Is a Message Ecosystem?

It's the collection of:

- Emails
- Social posts
- Lead magnets
- Landing pages
- FAQs
- Templates
- Testimonials
- Referrals
- Follow-ups
- Proposals
- Outbound scripts
- Web copy

…that all tell the same story — just in different ways, and for different moments.

A strong ecosystem means:

- No more rewriting from scratch
- No more confused clients
- No more one-and-done messaging

Everything connects. Everything compounds.

3. The Golden Thread

Your ecosystem works when it's built around a clear central message — your golden thread.

"We help [this type of client] solve [this kind of problem] so they can [specific outcome]."

That message doesn't change — it just wears different outfits.

Examples:

In an email:

"This solves the slow-sales slump and gets new clients in weeks, not months."

In a proposal:

"You mentioned delays in lead generation — this fixes that by building a steady, low-cost pipeline."

On your homepage:

"Grow your business with messages that win work — not just likes."

Your job is to say the same thing… in as many clear, relevant ways as possible.

4. Build Once, Use Everywhere

Start by writing your core message in these formats:

A 1-line version (e.g. tagline or hook)

A 1-paragraph version (e.g. About section)

A 3-part version (Problem > Solution > Outcome)

Once you have these, you can adapt them into:

Email signatures
LinkedIn bios
DM replies
Case study intros
Sales scripts
Cold email openers
Proposal intros
Social media captions
Video scripts

The format changes. The message stays the same.

5. How to Reuse Without Sounding Repetitive

People don't notice repetition as much as you do.

What they do notice is inconsistency.

So, when you reuse messaging:

Tweak the phrasing

Change the angle

Match the context

Always link back to your golden thread

Example:

Proposal:
"This helps you get better-fit leads without paid ads."

Social post:
"You don't need to burn money on ads to grow — try this instead."

Email subject:
"A better way to get quality leads (no ad spend required)"

Same idea. Different surface.

6. The Power of Templates and Tools

Part of your ecosystem should include templates you can deploy fast:

Proposal templates

Intro email formats

Follow-up scripts

FAQ answers

Testimonial requests

Landing page copy starters

These save time — and preserve voice, structure, and clarity.

You don't grow by writing more.
You grow by writing smarter — and reusing what works.

7. Create Your Personal Messaging Library

Set up a simple doc or folder with:

Your top 5 value statements

Your best "which means that" phrasing

Case study summaries (in STAR format)

Objection-handling phrases

Call-to-action lines

Testimonials

Reusable paragraphs from your proposals or emails

This becomes your Million Dollar Message Vault.

You'll use it every day — especially when things get busy.

Exercise: Map Your Message Ecosystem

Identify your most-used message types:
– Emails? Proposals? Website? Socials? Cold outreach?

Pick your golden thread message:
– "I help [who] do [what] so they can [result]."

Write a short version for each format:

Email intro

Proposal hook

DM opener

Social post

Landing page headline

Save them in your Message Vault.

Now you have a toolkit — not just a one-off message.

8. What Happens When You Get This Right

Your message becomes instantly recognizable
Your brand voice stays strong across platforms
You write faster and more consistently
You create more leads — without more effort
You stop reinventing the wheel every time

Your ecosystem becomes your engine.

And it keeps working — even when you're not.

Where We Go From Here

You've built the machine. Now let's make it even more powerful.

Because what you say matters — but so does when and how you say it.

Next, we'll cover how to time, pace, and sequence your messaging — so you build momentum, not just noise.

Message Timing and Momentum

When to Say What

CHAPTER 24

Because the right words at the wrong time still won't land

1. Great Messaging Needs Great Timing

You can write the clearest, most compelling message in the world...
But if you send it at the wrong time?

It falls flat.

Messaging isn't just about what you say.
It's also about when you say it — and in what order.

This Chapter will show you how to create momentum with your message, not just moments.

2. The Buyer Isn't Always Ready (Yet)

Here's something most people forget:

Not everyone is ready to buy when they first see your offer.

In fact, most aren't.

They're just starting to explore.
They're waiting for budget.
They're unsure what they even need.

That's why timing matters.

If you pitch too soon, it feels like pressure.
If you wait too long, someone else gets the job.

The trick?
Use messaging that moves them forward — without pushing.

3. Understand the 4 Buyer Readiness Stages

Tailor your message to match where the reader is:

Unaware

They don't even know they have a problem.

Use messages that reveal the cost of staying stuck.
"If your proposals aren't getting replies, the problem might not be what you think…"

Problem-Aware

They know something's wrong — but not the cause.

Use messages that name the pain clearly.
"You're great at what you do — but if clients don't get it, they won't buy it."

Solution-Aware

They're looking for help — but comparing options.

Use messages that position you as the clearest choice.
"This isn't just about better words. It's about getting chosen."

Decision-Ready

They're nearly there — but need a nudge.

Use messages that reduce friction and risk.
"You can get started today — no commitment, no pressure."

Each message has a job.
Say the wrong thing at the wrong stage, and momentum stalls.

4. Sequence Builds Trust

Messaging works best in layers:

Attention — You show up. You get noticed.

Clarity — You explain what you solve.

Belief — You show proof that it works.

Action — You make it safe to say yes.

That might happen across:

A post → DM → proposal
A homepage → email → call
A video → reply → follow-up

Build your message like a staircase, not a leap.

Each step builds confidence.

5. Don't Overload Too Early

A big mistake?

Dumping everything too soon:

- Features
- Pricing
- Case studies
- Guarantees
- Timelines

It's too much, too early.

Instead, ask:

"What's the next thing they need to believe — and how can I help them do that?"

Pace your message based on what they're ready to hear.

6. Use Checkpoints, Not Chases

Instead of constant chasing ("Just checking in…"), use confident checkpoints:

"Just touching base — does this still feel like a fit?"

"Still happy to help if this is the right time."

"Let me know if this has moved down the list — I won't chase."

These remind. They don't pester.

And they keep the door open without losing posture.

7. When to Re-Engage Old Leads

Past conversations = future clients.

Here's when and how to follow up:

Trigger Points:

30–60 days after no response
When something in their market changes
When you launch something new
When you've added new proof or results

Re-Engagement Message:

"Hey [Name] — just thought of you when [insert relevant trigger].

This new approach might solve what we spoke about — want to take a look?"

Keep it short. Keep it useful.
You're not nagging — you're helping.

Exercise: Your 4-Stage Message Map

1. Choose one of your main offers.

2. Map out the four key messages you want your audience to see — in the order they should see them.

3. Plug those messages into your content plan, email sequence, or sales process.

You've just built a message flow that creates momentum before the first conversation even happens.

8. What Happens When You Get This Right

Clients feel led, not pushed
You stay front-of-mind without chasing
Every message feels relevant, not random
You reduce ghosting and indecision
You create a flow that ends in action

It's not about pressure.

It's about progress.

And your message is what makes it happen.

Where We Go From Here

You've built the engine. You've fueled the momentum.

Now it's time to bring it all together — every principle, every tool, every shift.

Let's close this first section of the book the same way you'll close more deals:

Clearly. Confidently. And with a next step.

Putting It All Together– Your Million Dollar Words in Action

CHAPTER 25

This isn't the end. It's the beginning of everything you write from now on.

1. You Don't Need More Time. You Need a Clear Message.

Most people wait.

They wait until they feel more confident.
They wait until the website is done.
They wait until they've "figured it all out."

Let's start with something most people miss.

The words you choose today can change your business tomorrow.

But not you, not now, because by no you are armed with words…

Not perfect words.
Just clear ones.

That's what we've built in this book by this point.

2. Let's Recap the Million Dollar Shift

Here's what you now know:

- People don't buy what you do — they buy what it does for them
- The words you use either move people forward or hold them back
- You don't need to be the best — just the clearest
- "Which means that…" is one of the most powerful tools in business writing
- Quotes tell. Proposals sell.
- Voice isn't about being clever. It's about being consistent.
- Formatting, pacing, tone, and timing matter — because decisions are emotional first, logical second
- You already have enough experience to sound confident. Now you have the tools.

If it's not landing yet, don't go looking for better clients.

Go looking for better words.

3. This Book Was Built for Use — Not Just Insight

You haven't just read theory.

You've:

- Written stronger headlines
- Reframed your offers
- Crafted clearer proposals
- Improved your follow-ups
- Built your message library
- Structured better testimonials
- Sharpened your call to action
- Found a voice worth listening to

And now?

It's time to put those Million Dollar Words to work.

4. Section 2 — Where the Tools Live

The next section of this book is your execution kit.

This section turns everything we've learned into:

Templates you can use

Scripts you can send

Tools you can trust

Results you can repeat

Think of it as the practical layer — built to get you moving fast.

5. You're Now Part of a Bigger Conversation

If you've made it this far, you're not just interested in getting better at writing.

You're interested in being understood.
In being chosen.
In showing up with more clarity, more conviction, and more impact.

You're not alone.

Join us inside the Million Dollar Words Skool group — where we apply these principles to real businesses, with live support, templates, critiques, and more.

It's not a course.
It's a community of action.

Your next step is waiting there.

skool.com/million

6. Final Word

Before you carry on into the reference sections of the book it is worth restating that this book wasn't written to impress.

It was written to work.

To give you something better than clever — something clear.
To give you something better than content — something useful.
To give you the tools to make your message stand up, stand out, and get chosen.

So take what's here.
Use it.
Share it.

Return to it often.

And whenever you doubt what to say?

Just ask:

"What do they need to know — and what happens next?"

That's where your Million Dollar Words begin.

Turn the page to Section 2 — Put It Into Practice

Because now, it's time to do just that.

Section 2

PUT IT INTO PRACTICE

INTRODUCTION TO SECTION 2

Templates, tools, and examples you can use.

The first half of this book gave you clarity.
Now it's time to put it to work.

This section is your execution kit — practical, direct, and built for action.

Inside, you'll find:

Templates you can fill in

Phrases that land harder

Structures that save you hours

Scripts that get responses

Don't try to do everything at once.
Pick the part that solves your next challenge — and start there.

This isn't here for inspiration.
It's here to help you win more work, right now.

Let's get to it.

PUT IT INTO PRACTICE

Part 1: The Million Dollar Phrase Bank

Say it better. Mean it more.

You've already met the phrase that powers this entire book:

"Which means that…"

It's simple. Direct. Repeatable.
And used well, it might just be the highest-earning phrase in your business.

But here's the point:
It's not about this phrase alone — it's about what it does.

It translates features into outcomes.
It answers the "So what?" test before your client even has to ask.
It makes sure every sentence is doing a job.

Why This Phrase Matters

Most businesses talk in features:

"We offer 24/7 support."
"All our work is guaranteed."
"We've been in business for 12 years."

All true.
All technically useful.
None of it, on its own, makes someone choose you.

But when you add a short bridge — a clear outcome — you change everything.

"We offer 24/7 support — which means that if something breaks at 3am, you don't have to wait until morning. We'll fix it while you sleep."

That's not just words.
That's value.

It connects what you do… to what they care about.

Say This Instead — Alternatives to "Which Means That…"

You don't have to use the same phrase every time. Here are powerful, natural substitutes that shift the focus to their result:

- "So you can…"

- "That means you…"

- "Giving you…"

- "Allowing you to…"

- "Enabling you to…"

- "Making it possible to…"

- "Helping you to…"

- "Ensuring you can…"

- "Freeing you up to…"

- "Putting you in a position to…"

- "Making sure you…"

- "Resulting in…"

- "Leading to…"

- "So that you…"

- "Delivering…"

- "Creating…"

- "Opening the door to…"

- "Meaning you..."

- "Which gives you..."

- "That provides you with..."

- "Allowing for..."

- "Bringing you..."

- "That translates into..."

- "Which turns into..."

- "Which adds up to..."

- "That adds..."

- "That builds..."

How to Use Them:

1. Read your website, proposal, or brochure aloud.

2. Every time you say something that makes you sound good, add one of these connectors.

3. Complete the sentence from the **client's point of view.**

Example:
"We respond within 24 hours" → **"...so you can get issues resolved before they escalate."**

Try reading your website or brochure aloud.
If you state something that makes you sound good, immediately ask yourself:

"Which means that...?"

And finish the sentence from their point of view.

The "So What?" Test

This is your filter which helps you answer the "Which means that...?" ask.

Every claim, feature, or credential you use should pass this question:

So what?

If you say:

"We've been around since 2008."

You must follow it with:

"...which means that we've seen it all — and know how to fix problems before they cost you."

This test helps you cut the empty words and expand what matters.

Real-World Examples

Example 1:

Before: "We include a full user manual."
After: "We include a full user manual — so your team never has to guess what to do next."

Example 2:

Before: "We're ISO 9001 certified."
After: "We're ISO 9001 certified — which means we've proven we can deliver consistent quality, even under pressure."

Example 3:

Before: "We're not the cheapest."
After: "We're not the cheapest — but we are the safest pair of hands when you need things done properly."

This isn't spin.
This is perspective.

Watch Out For...

Filler outcomes like: "...which means you get a great service."
Be specific. Tangible. Practical. Human.

Making it all about you:

"We've won 5 awards — which means we're the best."
Flip it:
"We've won 5 awards — which means you're trusting a team that's recognized for excellence."

What Good Looks Like

Let's take one feature and show how the phrasing upgrades its impact:

Feature: "We respond within 2 hours."

Try Saying This Instead...

Here are 10 outcome-focused bridges you can use right now:

"So you don't have to worry about..."

"Which helps you avoid..."

"Giving you the confidence to..."

"So your team can focus on..."

"Allowing you to get back to..."

"So things just work — without you chasing."

"That way, nothing slips through the cracks."

"So it's easy for you to…"

"Helping you stay ahead, not behind."

"So you can stop firefighting and start planning."

Use them. Mix them. Make them yours.

Your Turn: Apply It

Take 3 of your own features, claims or facts — and write the Million Dollar version underneath.

Want to go deeper? Join us as skool.com/million

One Last Thing…

This isn't just a writing tool.
It's a thinking tool.

When you use "which means that" and the "So what?" test well, you don't just sound better — you understand your own value better.

And once you do that, it becomes much easier to:

Price confidently

Sell without awkwardness

Package your offer clearly

Build trust instantly

This is the engine.
Now let's drive it into your proposal.

Next up: The Million Dollar Proposal Blueprint
We'll show you how to package your pitch so that people say:

"This just makes sense."

THE MILLION DOLLAR PROPOSAL BLUEPRINT

Don't send a price. Send a reason to say yes.

Why Most Quotes Get Ignored

Let's be blunt.

Most quotes are:

Boring

Confusing

Hard to compare

Missing the "why now?"

And focused entirely on what they're offering — not why it matters

They look like this:

Quote
• Website build – $1,200
• Hosting – $120/year
• Email setup – $90
TOTAL: $1,410

That's a price list. Not a proposal.

And while it might be technically accurate… it's forgettable. And worse — it leaves the door wide open for the client to shop around.

But when you write a proposal using Million Dollar Words, you shift the entire conversation:

From cost → to value
From supplier → to partner
From maybe later → to let's go

What a Proposal Really Is

A proposal isn't just a nicer quote.

It's a decision-making tool.

Its job is to:

Prove you understand their problem

Explain how you'll solve it

Show the value of solving it now

Make the next step easy and safe

And it should feel like it was written just for them — even if it's built from a repeatable system.

The 5-Part Proposal Structure

Here's the structure we've used to help businesses win real contracts, sales, and funding worth $millions.

1. What We Understand

Mirror their situation in their words. Show that you've listened.

Example:

You mentioned you've outgrown your current setup, and need a cleaner, faster website that's easier to manage. You also said you're frustrated with slow response times from your existing support team.

Why this works:

It shows you're not sending a generic pitch

It makes them feel seen

It creates an emotional hook — "Yes, that's exactly it."

2. What We Propose

Now lay out your offer — but frame it in outcomes, not tasks.

Weak:

We'll build you a new WordPress site, including 5 pages and mobile optimization.

Better:

We'll build you a clean, fast-loading website that works on all devices — so your clients can find what they need quickly, and you can update it yourself in seconds.

Why this works:

It answers "So what?"

It focuses on the result, not the method

It's easier to say yes to something that makes sense

Try saying:
"We'll [what you do] — so that [what they get]."

3. What It Costs

Yes, you still need the price. But now it's in context.

Example:

Total investment: $1,800

This includes design, development, mobile responsiveness, training, and 30 days of support after launch.

We offer flexible payment plans if needed — just ask.

Why this works:

"Investment" sounds intentional

Context justifies cost

Reassurance removes friction

4. What Happens Next

Guide them to a decision. Don't leave them wondering what to do.

Example:

If you're happy with this proposal, just reply with "Let's go" or book a 10-minute call using [link].

Once confirmed, we'll get your project booked in and send over the short onboarding form.

We can usually get started within 7 days.

Why this works:

It removes ambiguity

It sets expectations

It feels easy and actionable

5. Why Us

Close with a brief, confident reminder of why you're a smart choice.

Example:

We've helped over 200 small businesses simplify their websites, reduce client drop-off, and look more professional online — all without the usual faff.

You'll always know what's happening, when it's happening, and who's doing it.

Why this works:

Proof > promises

Rebuilds trust just before they decide

Sounds human, not salesy

A Complete Mini-Proposal Example

WHAT WE UNDERSTAND
You told us your current accountant feels reactive, not proactive. You want to stay compliant, yes — but more importantly, you want strategic insight that helps you plan better and sleep easier.

WHAT WE PROPOSE
We'll take over your bookkeeping, tax returns, and payroll — but more than that, we'll give you a monthly forecast, so you always know what's coming. No surprises. No jargon. Just clarity.

WHAT IT COSTS
Monthly support package: $325 + VAT
Includes full tax return, year-end accounts, payroll for up to 5 staff, and monthly forecast reports.

WHAT HAPPENS NEXT

Just reply to this email with "Yes" or book a quick 15-minute onboarding chat here: [link]
We'll send your welcome pack and get started this week.

WHY US

We're not a faceless firm — we're a small team who've helped 60+ business owners move from panic to peace of mind. We're responsive, strategic, and speak in plain English.

Your Turn: Build Your Own Proposal

Use the structure below to write your next proposal — even if it's just a test.

Bonus: Write one real proposal using this format and send it within the next 48 hours.
Then track: response time, tone, and close rate.

Want a fill-in-the-blanks version with multiple layout styles?

Join us as skool.com/million

Final Word on Proposals

If someone asks for "just a quote," don't take the bait.

Give them a proposal.
Because quotes get compared.
But proposals get chosen.

Next up: Supercharged Email Scripts
Where we show you how to write emails that get opened, read — and replied to.

SUPERCHARGED EMAIL SCRIPTS

Because no one ever said "yes" to the email they didn't open.

Why This Matters

Most emails don't fail because of bad grammar.
They fail because they:

Start with "just checking in"

Feel generic or desperate

Don't say what they want

Offer nothing worth replying to

And yet email is still one of the most underrated, high-leverage tools in your business.
It's your first impression. Your follow-up. Your close. Your comeback.

So, if you're going to write emails — they might as well win.

What Makes an Email Supercharged?

It's not about sounding clever.
It's about sounding clear, useful, and human.

A supercharged email has:

A subject line that sparks curiosity or relevance
A first line that earns the next one
A clear reason to read
A next step that feels safe and easy
Zero faffing, filler, or filler

Let's break it down.

Script 1: Cold Intro with a Warm Hook

Use when: Reaching out to someone for the first time — especially if you're offering a service or starting a conversation.

Subject: Quick idea for [name/their business]

Email:

Hi [Name],

Saw your recent [post/site/update] and it made me think — I've helped others in your position solve [specific problem], and I think there's a way to make [desirable outcome] easier for you too.

If you're open to it, I'd be happy to share a quick idea or two — no pitch.

Best,
[Your name]

Why it works:

Opens with relevance

Offers something, asks nothing

Sets up the conversation, not the sale

Script 2: The "We're Not the Cheapest — Here's Why" Email

Use when: You've sent a proposal and know price might be an objection.

Subject: Why we're not the cheapest (on purpose)

Email:

Hi [Name],

Just wanted to say — if price is the only factor, we won't win.

But the reason our proposal came out higher is simple: we don't just deliver X — we make sure it works, lasts, and saves you time long after the invoice.

That means fewer fixes, fewer missed deadlines, and no "sorry we can't help you" moments down the line.

Happy to talk more if you'd like to unpack it.

[Your name]

Why it works:

Reframes value without begging

Shows confidence and integrity

Puts the buyer back in a thinking mindset

Script 3: Ghosted Follow-Up

Use when: They've gone quiet. You've already sent a proposal or had a call.

Subject: Did I miss something?

Email:

Hi [Name],

Totally understand if priorities have shifted — or if it's a no for now.

Just didn't want to assume either way.

Shall I close the file, or is this still something you're looking to move forward with?

All the best,
[Your name]

Why it works:

Invites a no (Chris Voss style)

Removes pressure

Often gets a fast reply

Script 4: "Still Interested?" Nudge

Use when: They showed interest but didn't take action.

Subject: Still interested?

Email:

Hey [Name],

A while ago you mentioned wanting to [solve problem/do outcome].

Still something you're thinking about — or has it moved down the list?

Either way's fine — just wanted to check.

[Your name]

Why it works:

Friendly tone

Reminder of why they were interested

Easy exit or re-engagement

Script 5: The Post-Project Upsell

Use when: A job ends, but you want to continue working with them.

Subject: What we'd do next (if you're up for it)

Email:

Hi [Name],

Really enjoyed working on [project]. If you're open to it, I've got a few simple ideas for where we could take things next — based on what we learned.

No pressure — just thought I'd ask before we close the door completely.

Would you like me to send them over?

[Your name]

Why it works:

Anchored in past success

Asks permission before pitching

Positions you as a long-term partner

Write It Yourself: Mini Template

Here's a fill-in-the-blanks version for any short outreach:

Subject: [Curious hook or reference]

Hi [Name],

[1 sentence about them — what you noticed, what they do, what they need.]

[1 sentence about how you might help — not a pitch, just a nudge.]

If it's worth chatting, happy to share a quick idea or two.

[Your name]

Common Mistakes to Avoid

Opening with "I just wanted to..."
Say what you mean. Own your message.

No subject line relevance
Use curiosity, benefit, or their name.

Too long
Aim for under 100 words. Respect attention.

Asking for time without offering value
Flip it: offer value, then ask for time.

Your Turn: Build a Mini Campaign

Pick a lead you haven't followed up with. Write a 3-email sequence:

Friendly re-intro

Proposal value reframe

Ghosting follow-up

Use the scripts above or modify with your own voice.

Then send them over 7–10 days.

Track:

Open rates

Replies

Outcomes

You'll be surprised how many "dead leads" weren't dead — just waiting for a better message.

Want all of these in one document, editable and ready to use?

Join us as skool.com/million

Final Thought

Emails are not just messages.
They're moments.

If you treat them as small, they'll work small.
But if you use the right words — they can open big doors.

Next up: The Value Reframe Builder
Where we turn "we offer…" into "you get…" — and help you say what your client really wants to hear.

THE VALUE REFRAME BUILDER

Turn features into outcomes — in minutes.

Why Most Messaging Misses the Mark

People don't buy what you do. They buy what it does for them.

But most businesses still write like this:

"We offer weekly reporting and remote access to your dashboard."

OK... but so what?

"We offer weekly reporting and remote access to your dashboard — so you're always in control and never waiting for an update."

That's a value reframe.

It's the art of taking something you already do — and expressing it in terms the buyer feels.

What is a Value Reframe?

It's a simple 3-part structure:

Think of it as a translation tool. You speak fluent features — your buyer speaks fluent outcomes. This is the bridge.

The Formula

We [do/offer/include]...
which means that...
so you can / so you don't have to / so it's easier to...

Example:

"We include onboarding and training — which means that your team is up and running from day one, with no costly delays or learning curve."

Common Mistakes

Listing features as if they're benefits

"We use cloud-based software." (OK... and?)

Reframe it:

"We use cloud-based software — which means that you can log in securely from anywhere, anytime — without waiting for files to be sent."

Saying "we're passionate" or "high quality" with no substance
Show what that means for them.

"We take quality seriously — so your job gets done right first time, every time."

Real-World Examples (Good → Better → Best)

Value Reframe Builder Table

Here's your fill-in-the-blanks worksheet — do this with 3–5 of your core offers.

Tip: Don't try to be clever. Be clear.

10 Useful Bridges You Can Use Instead of "Which Means That..."

Sometimes variety helps. Try these phrasing shifts:

"So you don't have to..."

"Helping you avoid..."

"Allowing you to…"

"That way…"

"Giving you…"

"Designed to ensure…"

"Built to help you…"

"So you can focus on…"

"Which helps you…"

"So it's easier for you to…"

Use whichever feels most natural. The goal is always the same: Shift the spotlight from what you do → to what they get.

Your Turn: Mini Exercise

Pick one of your own service lines or product features and write it three ways.

Now do that again with two more offers. Don't stop until it feels true and useful.

Bonus Challenge

Take your homepage or main sales email and highlight every time you talk about yourself (e.g. "We offer…" "Our service…" "We believe…")

Then rework those sentences using this structure:

"We [do]… which means that you [get]."

If the result feels more human and more helpful — you're doing it right.

Want a digital version of this table to reframe all your messaging?

Join us as skool.com/million

Final Word

The value is already there.
You don't need to invent anything.

You just need to show it clearly, confidently, and through the eyes of your buyer.

And that's exactly what a Value Reframe does.

Next up: Testimonial and Case Study Builder
Where we show you how to collect proof that speaks for itself — and structure it to win the next client.

THE TESTIMONIAL & CASE STUDY BUILDER

Proof sells. Here's how to make it powerful.

The Problem with Most Testimonials

"Great service."
"Lovely team."
"Would use again."

You've seen these.
You've probably written some of them for other people.
But the truth is:

These are nice — not useful.

They don't answer real doubts.
They don't highlight real results.
They don't help the next client say yes.

A good testimonial shows the person is happy.
A great testimonial shows the reader why they will be happy too.

And a case study? That's a testimonial with teeth.

Why This Matters

When you make bold claims, prospects wonder:

"Can you prove it?"

And when you don't make bold claims, prospects wonder:

"Why not?"

Strong, structured social proof helps:

Reduce buyer anxiety
Build credibility without bragging
Highlight outcomes without sounding salesy
Shorten the decision-making cycle

Part 1: Building a Better Testimonial

Don't ask for "a testimonial."
Ask better questions — and structure the answers.

Here's the Million Dollar 5-Part Prompt:

What problem were you facing before we worked together?

Why did you choose us over others?

What changed as a result of working with us?

What result surprised you most?

Would you recommend us — and why?

Send this as a short form, a casual email, or ask over a call. You'll get gold.

Weak vs Strong Example

Weak Testimonial:

"Alan was really helpful. Great communication and got the job done."

Strong Testimonial (Structured):

"We'd struggled to win any local contracts for over a year. Alan helped us completely reframe how we talk about our service, and within six weeks we landed a contract worth $48,000. What really surprised me was how simple the changes were — I'd recommend him to anyone who feels like their business is being overlooked."

Common Mistakes

Asking for a "review"
Ask questions that bring out the story

Publishing quotes with no context
Add a headline or intro to frame the quote

Hiding proof in the footer
Use it near your offer, price, or CTA

Exercise: Build Your First Testimonial

Pick one happy client. Ask them the 5 questions above.
Then draft the testimonial as a short story. Example structure:

"Before working with [you], we were [problem].
We chose you because [reason].
Since then, [change/result].
What really stood out was [surprise].
We'd recommend you because [reason]."

Part 2: The STAR(D) Case Study Format

A case study is different.
It's not about praise. It's about proof.

You're not just saying "Look how good we are."
You're saying "Here's how we solved a problem just like yours."

That's powerful.

The STAR(D) Structure

Example Case Study

Situation: A small facilities company was struggling to win local authority work — despite having years of experience.

Task: Help them write a clear, winning proposal for a school cleaning tender.

Action: We repositioned their offer, rewrote key answers, and provided social value prompts using our internal templates.

Result: They were shortlisted, interviewed, and awarded a $126,000 contract.

Demonstrates: That even small service-based businesses can win big public sector contracts — if they show the value properly.

Case Study Quick Builder

Pro tip: Keep each section to 1–2 sentences. Clarity > Detail.

Where to Use These

You don't need to "save" your best proof for the footer.

Here's where to put testimonials or case studies:

Right after the price — to reframe value

In your proposal — to overcome common objections

On your homepage — next to your offer

In your email footer — if short and sharp

In a PDF deck — to prove outcomes, not just logos

Want editable testimonial prompts and case study formats?

Join us as skool.com/million

Final Word

A good testimonial says:

"They were great."

A great testimonial says:

"They helped me do something that matters."

And a well-written case study does something even more powerful:

It makes the next person see themselves in your story —
and say "That's what I need too."

Next up: Before-and-After Copy Clinic
Where we take weak words and show you exactly how to rewrite them
for clarity, confidence, and conversion.

THE BEFORE-AND-AFTER COPY CLINIC

Because "professional service" isn't saying what you think it is.

Why This Matters

Every word you write is either building trust or wasting space.

Most businesses fall into one of two traps:

They use vague, empty language that sounds good but says nothing.

They describe what they do but never explain why it matters.

Either way — the reader doesn't get it.
And if they don't get it, they don't choose you.

But here's the good news:

Small changes in language can create huge shifts in how you're perceived.

That's what this clinic is about — showing you how to take what you already say… and say it in a way that actually works.

How to Spot Weak Copy

Here's your cheat sheet.

Million Dollar Rewrites (Real Examples)

Let's take a few of the classics and sharpen them.

Original:

"We offer a wide range of services to meet your needs."

Better:

"We help [target customer] solve [specific problem] — without the usual delays, jargon, or cost creep."

Original:

"We're experienced, reliable and friendly."

Better:

"We turn up on time, fix it first time, and explain what we've done without the jargon — so you're never left guessing."

Original:

"Our service is second to none."

Better:

"We've completed over 1,000 jobs with a 98% rebooking rate — and if we ever get it wrong, we make it right fast."

Original:

"We're passionate about helping our clients succeed."

Better:

"We don't just send reports — we tell you what to do next, what to fix, and what's working. That's why clients stay with us for years."

Try This Instead — 20 Overused Phrases and Stronger Upgrades

Overused Phrase	Stronger, More Specific Upgrade
We're passionate about [X]	We've delivered [specific result] for [number] clients in the last year — and we're ready to do the same for you.
We pride ourselves on quality	Every project goes through a [X]-point check before it reaches you.
We go the extra mile	If something's not right, we fix it within 24 hours — no charge.
We offer innovative solutions	We solved [specific challenge] for [client/industry] in [timeframe], saving them [X]%.
We have excellent customer service	When you call, you get your account manager — not a call center queue.
We're results-driven	Our last [project/service] increased [client metric] by [X]% in [timeframe].
We provide bespoke/tailored services	We start with your exact requirements, then build a plan around them — no templates.
We value our clients	Most of our clients have been with us for over [X] years.
We're industry-leading	Ranked in the top [X]% of providers by [credible source].
We understand your needs	Before starting, we spend a full day on-site with your team to see exactly what's working — and what's not.

Overused Phrase	Stronger, More Specific Upgrade
Committed to excellence	Every job is signed off by a senior engineer before completion.
Cutting-edge technology	We use [specific tool/tech] that reduces processing time by [X]%.
Trusted by clients nationwide	We currently work with [X] active clients across [list of regions/cities].
Experienced team	Our team has a combined [X] years' experience in [specific area].
Full-service provider	From initial design to aftercare, we handle everything in-house.
Customer-focused approach	We run quarterly review meetings to check progress and make improvements.
High standards	Our work meets or exceeds [industry standard/regulation] every time.
Reliable partner	98% of our projects are delivered on or ahead of schedule.
Flexible service	You can scale your plan up or down with just 48 hours' notice.
Proven track record	We've completed [X] successful projects in the last [timeframe].

How to Use This Table:

- Take your existing proposal, brochure, or website.
- Search for any of these overused phrases.

- Swap them for a **specific, measurable, and verifiable** upgrade.

Your Turn: Rewrite Your Own Copy

Choose 3 lines from your website, brochure, or LinkedIn profile. Then rewrite them using this formula:

[Claim] → [Specific Proof or Outcome]

Tip: If you can't prove it, don't write it.
If you can prove it — write that instead.

Common Mistakes

Using jargon to sound impressive
Use plain English to sound clear and trustworthy

Saying what everyone else says
Say what only you can say — or say it better than they do

Claiming quality without proof
Back it up with a result, stat, or story

Framing Your Benefits Like a Pro

Sometimes a single tweak unlocks the message:

Instead of: "We design logos for small businesses"
Try: "We give small businesses a visual identity they're proud to show off — and that clients remember."

Instead of: "We offer cleaning services to landlords"
Try: "We help landlords keep their properties tenant-ready — fast, clean, and without complaints."

That's what Million Dollar Words do:
They don't just describe. They connect.

Exercise: Your Messaging Makeover

Choose one of these key assets:

Your homepage

Your LinkedIn headline

Your Instagram bio

Your service page

Your About section

Now rewrite the first two sentences using:

Clear outcome
Specific proof
Emotional hook (optional)

Use this format:

"We help [who] solve [what problem] — so they can [what outcome]."

"Clients choose us because [specific reason or proof]."

Want a Full Walkthrough?

We've created a complete swipe file of weak → strong phrases across industries.

All you have too do is join us as skool.com/million

Final Word

Your words don't need to be flashy.
They just need to land.

Clear wins. Vague loses. Always.

Rewrite one sentence today.
Then one more tomorrow.
Your whole business starts to feel sharper — and so do you.

Next up: The Messaging Scorecard
Where we give you a fast, powerful way to self-check your copy before
it goes out the door.

THE MESSAGING SCORECARD

A 10-question gut check to see if your message is working.

Why Your Message Might Be Missing

You've written the page.
You've sent the proposal.
You've posted the offer.

And then… silence.

No click. No call. No reply.

It's not because you're bad at what you do.
It's usually because your message was too vague, too safe, or too hard to follow.

Most of the time, your offer is fine.
It's your words that are getting in the way.

That's where the Messaging Scorecard comes in.

What This Is

This is a fast, brutal, honest filter.

It tells you — in 5 minutes or less — whether what you've written is:

Clear

Useful

Believable

Persuasive

If it is, great. Ship it.

If not, fix it before it costs you another lead.

Who It's For

This scorecard is for:

Websites that sound OK… but aren't converting
Proposals that get "ghosted"
Sales emails that feel a bit flat
Social media bios or posts that aren't landing
Anyone writing about what they do — and wondering why it's not working

The 10-Point Messaging Scorecard

Clarity

    i.   Do I understand what you do in the first 10 seconds?

    ii.   Do you use plain English — not jargon or padding?

    iii.   Is the first sentence about me (the reader), not just about you?

    iv.   Have you explained the outcome — not just the feature?

    v.   Does every key statement pass the "So what?" test?

Credibility

    v.   Is there at least one specific piece of proof (e.g. stat, result, quote, client name)?

    vi.   Have you included a testimonial, case study, or success story?

    vii.   Do you avoid vague claims like 'high quality' or 'bespoke' with no evidence?

    viii.   Does the tone feel confident — not apologetic, generic, or overhyped?

    ix.   Is there a clear next step that feels easy, safe, and sensible?

Your Turn: Score Yourself

Take one real piece of messaging — your homepage, a recent email, a proposal, your About section, anything.

Now answer yes or no to each of the 10 questions above.

Count your total number of "yes" answers:

Example Fixes: Line-by-Line

Before:

"We offer bespoke services tailored to your business."

Sounds nice. Says nothing.

After:

"We help tradespeople and service-based businesses win better work — without spending a penny on ads."

→ Outcome-based.
→ Audience-specific.
→ Jargon-free.
→ Passes the "So what?" test.

Most Common Red Flags

"We pride ourselves on…"

"A range of tailored solutions…"

"Dedicated to excellence…"

"Innovative and forward-thinking…"

"Your one-stop shop for all your needs…"

These are not bad intentions. But they are bad messages.
They don't say what you do. They don't say why it matters. And they don't help you stand out.

What Good Messaging Feels Like

It's not clever.
It's not poetic.
It's not even "creative."

It's clear. Direct. Confident.

"I get what you do."
"I see how it helps me."
"I know what to do next."

If your reader thinks that — your message is doing its job.

Exercise: Quick Fix Audit

Pick one page of your website (or one recent proposal/email/post).

Now ask:

Where am I using vague or padded language?

Where am I making a claim I haven't backed up?

Where have I said what I do — but not what it delivers?

Make just three small changes:

Add a proof point

Rewrite one sentence with "which means that…"

Clarify the next step

You'll feel it immediately.
So will your reader.

Prefer a printable version?
We've made a clean 1-pager you can pin to your wall or share with your team.

All you have to do to get it is join us as skool.com/million

Final Word

You don't need more words.
You need better ones.

This scorecard helps you see what's working, what's missing, and what to fix.

Run every piece of messaging through it.
Especially the ones that feel right — but aren't getting results.

Next up: Quick Wins for Fast Impact
You've done the deeper work. Now let's look at the high-leverage moves you can make today — in 30 minutes or less.

QUICK WINS FOR FAST IMPACT

Make your message stronger — today, not someday.

Why You Don't Need More Time

You're busy.
You're juggling client work, admin, pricing, delivery, life.

So fixing your messaging?
That gets pushed to the bottom of the list.

Here's the shift:

You don't need hours.
You need ten minutes and the right move.

This part of the book gives you quick, strategic changes that sharpen your message fast.
No overhauls. No waiting. No filler.

What Counts as a "Quick Win"?

A quick win is a small change that creates one of these results:

 Makes you sound clearer
 Makes you easier to trust
 Makes you more relevant to the right person
 Makes it easier to say yes

You can do these on your lunch break. Or while waiting for a Zoom to start.

Let's go.

5-Minute Fixes

Rewrite Your Email Signature

Old:

"Regards, Jane Smith
Director, Acme Solutions Ltd"

New:

"Jane Smith | Helping local businesses save time on accounting
Free 15-min call: [link]"

Now every email becomes a mini pitch.
No more wasted real estate.

Add a "Which Means That..." Line to Your Homepage

Find the first bold claim on your site and add a second sentence:

"We manage your projects end to end — which means that you don't waste time chasing updates or correcting mistakes."

Simple. Powerful. Trusted.
Shifts focus from you to them.

Swap Your LinkedIn Headline

Old:

"Founder | Speaker | Marketing Consultant"

New:

"I help consultants win better work — with clearer messaging and stronger proposals."

Outcome over ego.
Attracts the right people instantly.

15-Minute Wins

Reorder Your Service Page

Put the result first.

Old:

"Our web design package includes hosting, updates, and mobile optimization."

New:

"We build websites that get you seen — fast, mobile-friendly, and easy to update."

Lead with the benefit.
Then explain the "how."

Add Proof to a Claim

Scan your site for these phrases:

"Trusted by businesses across the UK"

"High-quality service"

"Experts in our field"

Now add:

A stat

A client name (with permission)

A testimonial

A result

Example:

"Trusted by 63 Lancashire businesses — including 8 local councils."

Proof beats polish. Every time.

Turn One Testimonial Into a Mini Case Study

Original:

"Really helpful. Sorted the issue quickly."

New:

"We were struggling with invoicing delays and getting pressure from clients. Within 2 weeks, they set up an automated system that saved us hours — and removed a huge source of stress."

Story. Emotion. Outcome.
Built using the STAR(D) format from Part 5.

30-Minute Wins

Create a One-Liner That Works

Use this formula:

"We help [who] solve [what problem] — so they can [what outcome]."

Example:

"We help trades and service-based businesses win better work — without spending a penny on ads."

Now you've got something for your homepage, pitch, bio, and intro call.

Write a "Why Us" Box

Put it in your proposal or website footer:

Why People Choose Us:
- No copy-paste quotes
- 48-hour turnaround
- Named point of contact
- 4.9 stars from 137 clients
- If we ever get it wrong — we fix it. Fast.

Builds trust.
Feels real.
Easy to do today.

Rewrite Your Call to Action

Old:

"Contact us today."

New:

"Let's find out if this is a good fit — no pressure."
or
"Book a 10-minute call — we'll give you two ideas whether you hire us or not."

Removes risk.
Makes the next step feel obvious.

Try This: Pick One From Each Column

You don't need to do everything.
You just need to do something.

The Real Goal Here

These small changes are signals.
They say:

"We've thought this through."
"We care about clarity."
"We're serious — and safe to choose."

That's what your client wants. Not more noise — just a reason to
believe.

Want the Full Checklist?

We've created a Quick Wins worksheet — with 30+ fixes across pages,
emails, social, and proposals.

To get your free copy join us at skool.com/million

Final Word

The first draft is never perfect.
But every time you sharpen a sentence, replace a vague claim, or clarify
a result — you make it easier to win.

You don't need to change everything.
You just need to make it make sense.

One line. One change. One better outcome.

That's a Million Dollar Word.

That's the end of Section 2.
You've now got the tools, templates, rewrites and scorecards to build a
message that works — clearly, quickly, and repeatedly.

Section 3

SAY IT EVERYWHERE

INTRODUCTION TO SECTION 3

A quick-reference guide for real-world messaging.

By now, your message is sharper.
Now it's about showing up clearly — wherever it counts.

This section isn't about re-explaining the concepts.
It's about applying them: quickly, confidently, and consistently.

You'll find real-world examples and fast checks for:

Websites

Proposals

Social posts

Sales conversations

Email sequences

Testimonials and more

Come here when you're writing, revising, or just sense something's off.

It's your shortcut. Your cross-check.
Your way to make sure every message still does what it's supposed to:

Help the right people say yes.

SAY IT EVERYWHERE

Part 1: From Online to In Person — Keeping Your Message Consistent

Your message is your reputation. Say it the same, everywhere.

Why Consistency Beats Creativity

You don't need 12 versions of your message.
You need one message that adapts to the moment — without changing its meaning.

Most businesses make one of two mistakes:

They say something different on every platform.

They say the same thing the same way — even when it doesn't fit the context.

Both weaken your message.
Because if people can't repeat what you do, they can't remember it.
And if they can't remember it — they won't choose it.

The Golden Rule of Message Consistency

Your message should sound like you — no matter where it shows up.

That means whether someone sees you:

On your website

In your Instagram bio

In a proposal

Or hears you at a networking event...

...they should hear the same voice, feel the same confidence, and get the same idea of what you do — and why it matters.

The Core Message: Your Anchor Point

Let's go back to your one-liner from Section 2, Part 4:

"We help [who] solve [what problem] — so they can [outcome]."

That's your anchor.
Everything else builds around it.

Now let's see how it shows up differently in different places — without losing clarity.

Real-Life Example

Let's say your core message is:

"We help trades and service businesses win better work — without spending a penny on ads."

Now watch it flex — without breaking.

Website Hero Line:

Get Found. Get Chosen. No Ads.
We help local trades win better work — with sharper words and smarter proposals.

Email Signature:

Jane | Helping trades win more work without more marketing
Book a free 15-minute idea call → [link]

Instagram Bio:

Helping service businesses win without ads.
Tips, templates + messaging that gets results.

Sales Call (spoken aloud):

"In simple terms, I help small service businesses win better work —
often with the same offer, just packaged and positioned differently."

Proposal:

What We Understand:
You want to win more of the right work — but without spending more
time or money chasing it. That's exactly what we help with.

Same core message.
Different wrapper.
Consistent impact.

Where Consistency Falls Apart

Here's what to watch for:

Exercise: The Consistency Check

Pick three of these:

Website homepage

Instagram or LinkedIn bio

Email signature

Sales script

Proposal intro

Networking pitch

About page

Now ask:

Do they all say what I do — in the same basic language?

Do they sound like the same person wrote them?

Is the outcome I offer clear and consistent across each?

Could someone repeat this to a friend — and get it roughly right?

Where you say "no" — fix it.
One phrase at a time.

Pro Tip: Make It Repeatable

Here's the real power move:

Write your core message as if someone else had to sell you in 10 seconds.

If your message is clear enough for them to repeat — it's clear enough to win.

And when your website, your proposal, your pitch, and your posts all echo the same idea…
…it doesn't feel like marketing.
It feels like confidence.

Final Word

You don't need to reinvent your message for every platform.
You need to reapply the same truth — in context.

Consistent. Flexible. Recognizable.
That's how people trust you — before they've even met you.

Next up: Websites That Win Work (Not Awards)
Where we show you how to apply Million Dollar Words to your
homepage, about page, and services — so visitors stop scrolling and
start booking.

WEBSITES THAT WIN WORK (NOT AWARDS)

Because you don't need more traffic. You need more trust.

Why Your Website Isn't Working (Yet)

Most small businesses don't have a traffic problem, although traffic matters but even if you do get traffic to your website – most, and probably yours, have a conversion problem. Now I am not an expert at web design or SEO but the following when implemented can definitely help. So, here is what happens....

People land on your site.
They look around.
And then... they leave.

It's not because they weren't interested.
It's because your message didn't hit fast or clearly enough.

A website should just not a brochure.
When utilized properly it is also a decision tool.

It should answer three questions in the first 10 seconds:

What do you do?

Who is it for?

Why should I care?

If your homepage can do that, you're already ahead of 90% of businesses.

The Million Dollar Website Strategy: 3 Core Pages

You don't need 12 tabs and a parallax scroll.
You need three pages with clear outcomes:

Homepage — clarity and trust

About — empathy and authority

Services — offer and action

Let's break them down.

Page 1: The Homepage — What You Do and Why It Helps

What It's For:

Landing a first impression

Stating what you do, for whom, and why it matters

Getting the visitor to take the next step

What To Include:

A clear headline — not a slogan
A subhead that spells out the benefit
A short problem statement that shows you understand them
A proof point or result
A clear, low-friction call to action

Example Headline Formula:

We help [who] do [what] — without [common pain or hassle].

"We help small trades and service businesses win better work —
without spending a penny on ads."

Then follow up with:

Proof: "Used by over 60 local businesses across Lancashire."

CTA: "Book a free idea call — 15 minutes, no pitch."

Optional: One short testimonial underneath

Page 2: The About Page — Why You Get It

What It's For:

Showing you're human

Creating connection

Framing your experience around them, not just you

What To Include:

A short "why" — why you do this
A snapshot of your experience — but focused on what it helps them achieve
A key belief or principle that builds trust
A clear link back to the offer
One story, not a CV

Example Reframe:

Before:
"Founded in 2017, we have a passion for delivering tailored digital solutions to our clients across a range of sectors."

After:
"I started this because I saw too many brilliant tradespeople losing work to weaker competitors — simply because of how they talked about themselves. So I fixed the words. And they started winning."

Page 3: The Services Page — Offer and Action

What It's For:

Showing what you do, simply

Framing features as outcomes

Giving people a way to take the next step

What To Include:

One clear headline: "What We Offer"
2–3 services, each explained in outcomes not tasks
Pricing if possible — or at least "what's included"
One strong testimonial or case study
A simple CTA after each section

Example Service Description:

"Proposal Rewrites — We take your existing quote or bid and turn it into a proposal that gets chosen. Includes messaging overhaul, formatting, and clarity pass."

It's not about what you do.
It's about what they get.

What to Avoid

- Hero images with no headline
- Generic phrases like "Welcome to our site" or "solutions for your business"
- Walls of text10+ menu items and no clear path to act
- A "Contact Us" button with zero context

You don't need to be fancy.
You need to be findable, believable, and clear.

Quick Exercise: The Homepage Health Check

Read your homepage aloud and ask:

Does it say who I help — and how — in the first 10 seconds?

Is the benefit to them clear and visible?

Do I have any stats, proof, or client names visible without scrolling?

Is my CTA easy to find — and low commitment?

Can someone say "yes" to me without having to talk to me first?

If not — rewrite one section.
Use a headline from this book. Or borrow one from your best-performing proposal.

Optional: Wireframe Layout (for illustration)

If we were drawing this on a whiteboard, your homepage would look like this:

[Clear Headline]

[Subhead with Benefit]

[CTA Button]

[Short Problem Paragraph]

[3 Bullet Benefits]

[Visual or Icon Line]

[Testimonial or Stat Line]

["Why Us" Box]

[Simple Services Preview]

[Final CTA + Contact Link]

Not pretty. But effective.

We can add this as a visual in the final print version — simple black-and-white, hand-drawn style.

Final Word

Your website is not for you.
It's for the person making a decision.
They're asking:

"Do I get it?"
"Do I believe it?"
"Do I want to take the next step?"

If your site answers those clearly — you win.

Next up: Proposals, Pitches, and the Power of Simplicity
Where we show you how to take the Million Dollar approach into live bids, presentations, and high-stakes meetings — without overcomplicating your message.

PROPOSALS, PITCHES, AND THE POWER OF SIMPLICITY

When the stakes are high, your words need to land — not impress.

Why People Overcomplicate When It Matters Most

You finally get the meeting.
You're invited to pitch.
You're shortlisted for the contract.

And then…
you throw everything you've got at the page or the room.

Fancy slides
Every credential you can find
A paragraph where a sentence would do
Bullet points. Then more bullet points.
Diagrams that no one asked for

It's not that you're wrong.
It's that you're overloading the buyer with information — instead of making a confident case.

The Real Job of a Proposal or Pitch

It's not to explain everything.
It's to make them say, "This is the right fit."

Your job isn't to sound smart.
It's to sound like someone who:

Gets the problem

Knows what matters

Can actually deliver

Won't disappear after the invoice

In a word: trust.

And trust is built on clarity, not complexity.

A Proposal is a Decision Document

If you take nothing else from this Chapter, take this:

A proposal isn't a description of what you do.
It's a tool to help someone say yes.

Stop writing like a lawyer, and start writing like a guide.

Let's walk through how to do that.

The Million Dollar Proposal Structure (Revisited)

You've seen this in Section 2. Now here's how to apply it under pressure — in bids, tenders, and presentations.

1. What We Understand

Restate their need in their words. Not yours.

Why it matters: It shows you've listened — and that this isn't a copy-paste job.

2. What We Propose

Lead with the outcome, not the process. Then show how you'll get them there.

Why it matters: It proves you're not just task-focused — you're result-driven.

3. What It Costs

Be clear. Be confident. Don't hide your pricing — frame it as the value of solving the problem.

4. What Happens Next

Lay out the steps. Make them feel in control. Remove ambiguity.

5. Why Us

Anchor your pitch in proof. Not filler. Not titles. Not buzzwords.

How This Changes in a Big Bid

When you're bidding for something more formal — like a public sector contract or a corporate RFP — here's what changes:

Example: Bid Answer Rewrite

Question:

"Please describe your approach to project delivery."

Weak Answer:

"We pride ourselves on a hands-on approach, managing projects to the highest standard, ensuring deadlines are met and client satisfaction is achieved."

Stronger Answer:

"We break delivery into 3 phases — mobilization, live delivery, and final sign-off.
In each phase, we assign one lead contact, use weekly status updates,

and provide a named escalation route.

Which means that your project stays on track — without needing to chase progress or fix missed steps.

This approach has helped us deliver 98% of projects on time, with 4.9/5 average feedback scores."

In the Room: Pitches and Presentations

When you're speaking — not writing — the principles are the same:

- Be clear.

- Be concise.

- Make it about them.

Here's how to apply the *Million Dollar* approach live:

1. Lead with the Outcome, Not the Agenda

Don't start with "Thanks for having me" and a slide about your company history.

Start with:

"If we work together, here's what you can expect in the next 90 days…"

2. Use the "Which Means That" Connector in Real Time

When you show a feature or stat, instantly connect it to their benefit:

"This software automates your invoicing — **which means** you can get paid in days, not weeks."

3. Structure Your Flow for Scanners

In writing, scanners look for bold headings.
In the room, scanners are *listeners with short attention spans.*
Break your talk into **three clear chunks** they can follow without notes.

4. Make Proof Tangible

Don't just say "We've helped other clients."
Say:

"Last year, we helped a company your size reduce project delays by 18% in four months."

5. Flag the Gold

Pause before the most important point. Change your tone. Slow down. Let them know:

"If you remember just one thing from today, it's this…"

6. Handle Questions with the 3-Part Answer

When they ask, "How would you handle X?":

1. **Acknowledge** ("Good question.")

2. **Answer** ("Here's how we approach it…")

3. **Anchor Back to Outcome** ("…so you can keep projects moving without extra cost.")

7. Close with the Next Step

Make it specific, low-risk, and easy to say yes to:

"If you'd like to go ahead, we can lock in the start date today and have the onboarding done by next week."

Pro Tip:
If you're nervous, build "checkpoint" slides or bullet cards with your three key points — so you never wander, and you always land on what matters most.

Exercise: Reframe Your Next Pitch

Pick one pitch, meeting, or proposal you've got coming up.

Then ask:

What's the core outcome they want?

What's the best proof you have that you can deliver it?

What's the clearest way to say that — in 1–2 sentences?

Where can you use "which means that…" to anchor it in their world?

Now build your answer, script, or slide around that.

Not what makes you sound smart.
What makes you sound right.

Final Word

When the stakes are high, your instinct will be to add more.

More slides.
More stats.
More buzzwords.

Fight that.

Say what matters. Say it clearly. Say it first.

The best proposals and pitches don't sound fancy.
They sound like clarity under pressure.
And clarity wins.

Next up: Email Sequences That Get Chosen
We'll show you how to make every message — from hello to follow-up
— work harder, land better, and lead to more yeses.

EMAIL SEQUENCES THAT GET CHOSEN

Not just opened. Not just read. Replied to.

Why Email Still Wins (If You Know What to Say)

It's not dead. It's not outdated. It's not "just noise."

Email, when done right, is still the most direct, trusted, and reply-worthy channel you've got.

But most emails die in the same three places:

The subject line — no one opens it.

The first sentence — no one keeps reading.

The call to action — no one replies.

Let's fix all three — and then build full sequences that convert.

The Big Shift: From Email as a Task → Email as a Journey

A single message is easy to ignore.
But a sequence — written with purpose, clarity and confidence — becomes:

A 'story', via a sequence of short 'chapters'
A strategy
A series of small yes's that lead to the big one

That's what we'll build here.

The Core Principles of a Million Dollar Email

Whether you're writing one or five, every message should be:

Short — no one reads essays
Clear — what's this about and why does it matter?
Helpful — offer value, not just information
Conversational — write like a person, not a company
Outcome-led — what do they get from this?

And above all: make it easy to say yes.

Sequence Structure: The 5 Email Journey

Let's build a simple but effective 5-email sequence. This could be used for:

Cold outreach

Proposal follow-up

Warm lead nurturing

Re-engagement

Email 1: The Problem Mirror

Subject: "Not sure if this is happening for you…"

Body:

Hi [Name],

A lot of [business owners like you] tell me they're doing great work — but missing out on better contracts because their message isn't landing.

If that's ever felt familiar, I've got one or two quick ideas that could help.

Want me to send them over?

Why it works:

Starts with empathy

Makes them feel seen

Offers something without pitching

Email 2: The Reframe and Tease

Subject: "The real reason good businesses get overlooked"

Body:

You don't need a better logo. Or a fancier website.

Most people just need clearer words.

Because if people don't get what you do — they don't buy it.

That's what I help with.

Want me to show you how your offer could be reframed to land better?

Email 3: The Mini Win

Subject: "Quick win — if you do one thing this week, do this…"

Body:

Here's something you can fix in 10 minutes that'll make a difference:

Take the first sentence on your homepage or LinkedIn bio and run it through this:

"So what?"

If it doesn't answer that, rewrite it with:

"We help [who] with [what] — so they can [benefit]."

Need help rewording it? Send it over. I'll take a look.

Why it works:

Delivers real value

Invites interaction

Positions you as helpful (not pushy)

Email 4: The Light Touch Follow-Up

Subject: "Is this still something you're thinking about?"

Body:

Totally understand if things have shifted.

Just didn't want to assume.

Still worth a quick conversation — or has it dropped down the list?

Why it works:

Low pressure

Invites a no

Reopens the loop without chasing

Email 5: The Close or Circle Back

Subject: "Shall I close the file?"

Body:

If now's not the right time, all good — just let me know and I'll stop nudging.

But if this still feels relevant, happy to chat or give some honest thoughts on where your messaging might be costing you work.

Why it works:

Respectful

Confident

Ends the thread with a gentle offer

Exercise: Build Your Own Sequence

Choose one of these:

Cold outreach

Follow-up from a proposal

Warm lead with no reply

Now draft a 3–5 email journey using this structure:

Empathy and observation

Reframe the problem

Deliver value

Nudge for clarity

Invite the yes or no

Even if they don't buy — they'll remember how you showed up.

Common Email Mistakes

"Just checking in…"
Instead: "Has anything changed since we last spoke?"

Overwriting
Keep it to 100–125 words

Asking for 30 minutes
Start with 10 — or offer a helpful idea instead

"Let me know if you're interested"
Try: "Want me to send over a few ideas?"

Million Dollar Phrases for Email CTAs

Here's a quick list you can use in any message:

"Want me to send that over?"

"Shall I take a look?"

"Is this still something you're thinking about?"

"Would it help if I showed you how that could look in practice?"

"Want me to build a draft to show you what I mean?"

"No pressure either way — but thought I'd ask."

Clarity. Relevance. Respect.

That's how email wins.

Final Word

Most people treat email like a task:
Write it. Send it. Wait.

Million Dollar email is different.
It's clear. Confident. Helpful. Timed.

It doesn't just fill an inbox.
It creates momentum.

And the more useful your email is — the less selling you ever have to do.

Next up: Social Posts That Get Saved, Shared, and DMs
Where we help you write social content that earns attention without shouting, builds trust without padding, and turns lurkers into leads.

SOCIAL POSTS THAT GET SAVED, SHARED, AND DMS

You don't need more content. You need more clarity.

Why Most Business Content Doesn't Land

You've seen it. You've probably posted it.

"Monday motivation"
"We're proud to have completed this project!"
"Here's our team in action!"
"Don't forget to follow us!"

It's not wrong. It's just not remembered.
It doesn't say anything meaningful — or make anyone stop scrolling.

The problem isn't frequency. It's focus.
Most content talks around the problem.
Million Dollar content talks straight through it.

What Makes Social Content Land?

Three things:

Hook — Get attention with relevance or emotion

Help — Give something useful, even in one sentence

Human — Show that a person wrote this, not a content calendar

That's it.

If your post does all three — it doesn't matter how long it is. It'll hit.

The Million Dollar Post Format: Hook → Help → Human

Let's look at each layer.

1. The Hook

This is the scroll-stopper. It could be:

A direct problem:

"Struggling to get replies to your proposal emails?"

A reframe:

"Most sales problems are messaging problems in disguise."

A contrarian truth:

"No one wants your 'tailored solutions.' They want to understand what you actually do."

A teaser:

"The phrase that's helped me (and my clients) win over $200 million…"

2. The Help

This is where you give something they can use or remember.

It could be:

A tip

A one-liner

A rewrite example

A list

A new way to look at something they thought they already understood

Example:

"Before: 'We offer professional service tailored to your needs.'
After: 'We show up on time, get it done right, and explain what we did
— so you don't have to chase or guess.'"

3. The Human

This is what gives your post tone, identity, and real-world weight.

It could be:

A short story

A specific moment or client

A self-aware sentence

A plain, spoken-style CTA (e.g. "Want me to send it over?")

"This stuff isn't clever. It's clear.
It's won my clients contracts, grants, and clients they thought were out
of reach.
If you want to see what this looks like in your world — send me your
homepage. I'll show you."

Examples: Million Dollar Posts That Work

LinkedIn

The biggest messaging mistake I see?
Writing like you're trying to win an award.

Your client doesn't want clever.
They want to understand you.

So here's the fix:
"We provide tailored business solutions" →
"We help [who] with [what] — so they can [outcome]."

That rewrite alone has helped clients win 5- and 6-figure work.
Want help doing yours?

 Hook = biggest mistake
 Help = rewrite template
 Human = client result + offer to help

Instagram

This phrase built my whole business:
"Which means that…"

It turns this:
"We offer weekend callouts."

Into this:
"We offer weekend callouts — which means you're not stuck waiting until Monday."

More helpful. More human. More chosen.

Save this one. You'll use it again.

Hook = "phrase built my whole business"
Help = rewrite demo
Human = instruction + tone

Try This: Plug and Post

Use this fill-in-the-blanks template to write a quick post today:

Most people [do X]…
But that's not what gets results.

Instead, try this:
"[Old version]" → "[New version with outcome]"

This has helped my clients [result].

Want help applying it to your [thing]?

Common Mistakes to Avoid

"Happy Monday! Just a quick update…"
Lead with the point. No one came for a calendar chat.

Paragraphs with no spacing
Break up your post so it's easy to scan

Sharing a photo with no message
Every visual still needs a verbal hook or takeaway

Overexplaining
Trust the reader. Say less — but say it clearly.

Exercise: Write One Post Using the 3-Part Formula

Pick one idea you care about — something you say to clients, or a phrase you wish more people understood.

Then write:

1 sentence hook

2–3 sentence helpful idea

1 human sign-off or story

Now post it.
See what lands.
Tweak it next time.

This is practice — not performance.

Final Word

You don't need to go viral.
You need to be valuable.

Social posts aren't about volume.
They're about visibility, clarity, and credibility.

The people who are ready — they're not liking.
They're reading.
And they're watching for someone who gets it.

Be that person.

Next up: Sales Conversations That Convert
Where we take everything you've written and show you how to speak it
— clearly, calmly, and confidently — in person, on calls, or in
meetings.

SALES CONVERSATIONS THAT CONVERT

Talk less. Say more. Win the work.

Why Saying It Out Loud Feels Harder

You've nailed the message on your website.
Your emails are sharp.
Your proposal lands well.

But then you're in a room.
Or on a call.
Or standing at a networking event.

And suddenly the words feel... slippery.

You ramble.
You hedge.
You explain too much — or not enough.
You leave the other person confused — or just polite.

The problem? You haven't yet built the spoken version of your message.

That's what this Chapter fixes.

What This Chapter Covers:

How to explain what you do — in one confident sentence
How to handle live objections with clarity
How to make outcome-driven conversation feel natural
How to invite a "no" without losing the sale
How to move from interest → yes, without pressure

This is not about slick persuasion.
It's about confident, clear, outcome-first talk.

The Real Goal of Any Sales Conversation

It's not to impress.

It's to help the other person feel safe, understood, and clear.

Because people don't say yes to the smartest pitch.
They say yes to the clearest one — from the person they trust to deliver.

Start With a One-Line Outcome

When someone says, "What do you do?" don't give them your job title.

Give them this:

"I help [who] do [what] — so they can [result]."

Examples:

"I help trades and service businesses win more work — without spending a penny on ads."

"I help small charities win funding — by making their bids more believable and their impact more visible."

"I help busy founders sharpen their message — so they stop being overlooked and start getting picked."

Keep it slow.
Keep it simple.
And then — stop talking.

Let them respond.

Handling the "Tell Me More" Moment

Here's what most people do next:

Word-vomit their full process, history, and client list.

Here's a better option:
Tell a short story of a win.

"One recent client was a domestic cleaning company. She was doing great work — but getting passed over for bigger jobs. We rewrote her pitch, helped her show her value clearly, and within a month she landed a contract with a lettings agency for 15 properties a week."

That's it.
Not a pitch — a picture.

Live Use of "Which Means That..."

In conversation, the spoken version still works:

"We take the whole application off your hands — which means that you don't need to spend your evenings trying to make sense of funding criteria or red tape."

or

"We build the proposal around your strengths — so when the client reads it, they're already picturing you doing the job."

Used right, it's one of the most trustworthy phrases in sales.
Because it translates features into outcomes — live.

Objections? Use This 3-Step Response

If they raise a concern — about price, timing, or fit — don't dodge it.

Instead, try:

Acknowledge it: "That makes total sense."

Reframe it: "Most people I work with felt the same at first."

Bridge it: "What changed for them was seeing how it actually saved time — not added more."

This is respectful. Strategic. Confident.

The Power of Inviting a No

This is one of the most powerful closes you'll ever use:

"Is there any reason this wouldn't be a good fit for you right now?"

It does two things:

If there is a reason — you hear it now, not later
If there isn't — you often get a clear yes, right there

It feels low-pressure.
But it leads to a real decision.

Exercise: Build Your Spoken Sales Stack

One-line answer to "What do you do?"

One short success story you can tell in under 30 seconds

One benefit you can explain with "which means that…"

One confident close you can use without pressure

"Is there any reason we couldn't move forward on this today?"
or
"Want me to show you what this would look like in your world?"

Now practice it out loud.
Yes, out loud.
You'll hear the difference in your own voice.

Common Mistakes to Avoid

Trying to sound too clever
Speak like you write — clearly, calmly, and confidently

Listing features
Always tie it to what it does for them

Apologizing for your price
Explain what's included and what it means — then stop

Pitching to fill space
Ask a great question, then listen

Final Word

You don't need a perfect pitch.
You need a true, useful message — delivered with confidence.

When you say it clearly, the right people lean in.
When you say it calmly, the right people trust you.
And when you say it in outcomes — the right people say yes.

Next up: Testimonials, Referrals and Reputation — Without Asking
Weirdly

We'll show you how to build social proof that spreads, referrals that feel natural, and a reputation that repeats itself — without awkward asks or needy energy.

TESTIMONIALS, REFERRALS, AND REPUTATION — WITHOUT ASKING WEIRDLY

Let other people say what you shouldn't have to.

Why Most People Struggle With Social Proof

You've done the work.
They're happy.
The results were real.

And yet…

"Could you write us a testimonial?"

"Would you mind leaving a review?"

"Can I ask a favor?"

It feels awkward.
So you put it off. Or worse — you get something like:

"Great service. Would definitely recommend."

Kind. Polite. Useless.

This Chapter is about changing the way you collect, trigger, and use proof — so that it works for you, without making it weird.

What We'll Cover:

How to get stronger testimonials — without asking for "a testimonial"
How to trigger referrals organically
How to make your message easier to repeat

How to use reputation to shorten the sales cycle

Where to use your best proof — so it's seen, not saved

Why Testimonials Work (When They're Good)

A testimonial isn't just a compliment.

It's a short story that tells your future client:

"This worked for me — it might work for you too."

The more specific the story, the more believable the result.

The 5-Question Testimonial Format

Never ask:

"Can you write me a testimonial?"

Ask these five questions instead:

    i.   What problem were you facing before we worked together?

   ii.   Why did you choose us?

  iii.   What changed as a result?

  iv.   What result surprised you most?

   v.   Would you recommend us — and why?

You can do this:

In an email

In a form

On a short call

Or turn it into a LinkedIn message prompt

Example Before and After

Before:

"Brilliant work. Would use again."

After (structured):

"I was trying to win public sector contracts but getting nowhere. Alan helped me completely reframe how I talked about my business. Within six weeks I landed a $48,000 contract — and felt way more confident doing it. I'd recommend him to anyone who feels like they're doing the work but not getting picked."

Problem
Process
Result
Emotion
Recommendation

Exercise: Trigger the Testimonial

Choose one recent client or customer.
Send them these five questions in plain English.

Then:

Tidy up their answers (don't change meaning)

Send it back for approval

Ask if you can use it on your site, proposal, or social

That's it.
No awkwardness.
Just structured success, in their own words.

Referrals Without the Ask

Good clients often want to refer you.
They just don't know how to explain what you do.

So make it easy. Try this:

"If you know anyone who's in the same boat you were in — feel free to pass them this message. You don't have to explain anything — just say I helped you get [outcome], and I'd be happy to help them too."

Removes the pressure
Makes it easy to repeat
Sounds like a favor, not a pitch

Bonus: Pre-Written Referral Blurb

You can even give them a copy-and-paste version:

"If you're trying to [do X] and want someone who can help without the filler — I recommend [Your Name]. They helped me [specific result] and were clear, honest, and quick."

Now you're not just being referred.
You're being introduced — with your message intact.

Building a Repeatable Reputation

You don't want to be remembered vaguely.
You want to be remembered for one clear thing.

So think of your message like a chorus:

"I help [who] do [what] — so they can [outcome]."

Say it in every email, pitch, post, and talk.

Now every happy client becomes an amplifier.
They repeat you the way you want to be repeated.

Where to Use Your Proof (Not Just Where You Think)

Not just at the bottom of your website
Not just in your proposal appendix
Not just on a lonely Trustpilot page

Use your best testimonial on the homepage
Drop a relevant case study in a pitch conversation
Put a referral story in your welcome email
Use one quote under your price in a proposal

Proof works best near the decision point — not hidden in a "nice to have" section.

Final Word

You shouldn't have to shout about yourself.
You should make it easy for others to tell the story.

Structure the story.
Place it where it counts.
Let your work do the talking — through them.

That's how proof becomes persuasion.

Next up: Building Your Messaging Library
Where we show you how to create a personal swipe file of your best lines, phrases, stories, and proof — so you never start from scratch again.

BUILDING YOUR MESSAGING LIBRARY

So you never start with a blank page again.

Why This Matters

You've done the work.
You've sharpened your message.
You've written clearer proposals, smarter emails, stronger posts.

But then a new opportunity comes up and you think:

"What do I say?"
"Where's that line I used before?"
"What did I write in that great pitch last month?"

This is where most businesses waste time and lose momentum.
They keep rebuilding their message — instead of saving what already works.

So let's fix that.

What is a Messaging Library?

It's your personal vault of phrases, lines, proof, and structure —
organized and ready to drop into:

Proposals
Emails
Web pages
Conversations
Slides
Ads

Social posts
Scripts
Pitches

Think of it like a swipe file — but made of your words, not someone else's.

What to Include in Your Library

Here's what to start collecting:

The goal is to build your own toolbox. Not to memorize — but to reuse, adapt, remix.

Where to Store It

Pick a place you'll actually use. It could be:

A simple Google Doc

A Notion database

A Notes app folder

A physical notebook if that's how your brain works

Label sections clearly. Add examples as you find them.
This isn't admin — it's leverage.

Your First 30-Minute Build

Start here:

Copy your favorite testimonial and drop it in

Write your core one-liner at the top

Add 3 "which means that…" reframes from past work

Paste in one subject line that got a reply

Write down your best answer to: "Why should I choose you?"

That's it. You've already built your foundation.

How to Use It in Practice

You're writing a proposal?
→ Go to your "proof points" and "CTAs" sections.

You're about to speak at a networking event?
→ Grab your "One-liner" and "Analogy" notes.

You're writing a new LinkedIn post?
→ Copy a format from "Headlines" or "Value Reframes."

This is how pros move faster.
They don't write better words — they reuse their best ones.

What Not to Do

Let it grow into chaos — no folders, no labels
Save things you'd never actually say aloud
Forget to update it — make time once a month
Hoard vague praise — save structured, useful proof

This isn't about saving everything.
It's about saving what works — so you can work smarter.

Want a Head Start?

We've created a blank Messaging Library template you can copy, fill out, and expand.

It's structured exactly as above — ready to go.

Final Word

Most people keep trying to reinvent their message.
The smart ones organize it.

Build your Messaging Library once.
Then use it forever.

Because you won't always have time to find the perfect words.
But if you've written them once — you never have to again.

That's the end of Section 3

You've now got the skills and systems to apply your Million Dollar Message across:

Your website

Your proposals

Your emails

Your social content

Your calls

Your client relationships

Your own library

From this point forward, every part of your business becomes sharper, stronger, and more strategic — simply by choosing better words.

AND FINALLY...

You Made It. Now Let's Put It to Work.

If you've made it this far, you're not just a reader. You're a builder.
You've done something most people never do — you didn't just dip in
for a quick tip or scroll through a summary.
You showed up. You stayed the course. You wanted to get chosen —
and now you've got the tools.

We covered a lot.
The words that weaken. The ones that win. The power of framing,
focus, timing, trust.
And the engine that drives it all: "which means that..."

But let's be honest — a book is just a start.

Your real edge comes from applying this stuff.
Sharpening your pitch. Rewriting that quote. Reframing how you talk
about what you do — every day, in real life, with real people.

That's where the next step comes in.

> If these pages have shifted how you see, feel, or decide, then you've
> already experienced Million Dollar Words. Now you get to decide what
> to do with them.

COME JOIN US

If this book landed for you, we've built something to take it further. It's called the Million Dollar Words Skool Group — and it's where this book comes to life.

We've got:

Live Q&As and community coaching

Deep dives and working sessions

Templates, toolkits, and cheat sheets

Real feedback from real people

And most of all — momentum and community of founders, owners and entrepreneurs just like you.

I am active in there virtually every day to support everyone I can.

You don't need another course. You need a home for this new way of thinking.

That's what we built.

Join us as skool.com/million

ONE SMALL ASK (THAT MAKES A BIG DIFFERENCE)

If this book helped you — even one sentence that hit just right — I'd love it if you'd leave a short review.

It doesn't have to be long or poetic. Just true.
Tell people what problem this helped you solve — and what changed for you after reading it.

Your words might help someone like you say:
"This is what I've been looking for."

Leave a review wherever you got the book from online or simply send an email to me

alan@milliondollarwords.info

We read every single one. And yes — they mean more than you know.

A QUIET NUDGE

You made it here.

You now know more about powerful communication than 99% of business owners.

The only question left is:

What will you say next?
And will it be worth a million dollars?

Let's stay connected.
Let's make words count.
Let's make work work!

Alan
Founder, Million Dollar Words

alan@milliondollarwords.info

Printed in Dunstable, United Kingdom

66714543R00178